THE PURITAN AND THE CYNIC

THE PURITAN
AND THE CYNIC
Moralists and Theorists in French and American Letters

Jefferson Humphries

New York   Oxford
OXFORD UNIVERSITY PRESS
1987

Oxford University Press

Oxford   New York   Toronto
Delhi   Bombay   Calcutta   Madras   Karachi
Petaling Jaya   Singapore   Hong Kong   Tokyo
Nairobi   Dar es Salaam   Cape Town
Melbourne   Auckland

and associated companies in
Beirut   Berlin   Ibadan   Nicosia

Published by Oxford University Press, Inc.,
200 Madison Avenue, New York, New York 10016

Oxford is a registered trademark of Oxford University Press.

Library of Congress Cataloging-in-Publication Data

Humphries, Jefferson, 1955–
The Puritan and the Cynic.

Bibliography: p.
Includes index.
1. French literature—History and criticism.
2. Ethics in literature.   3. Literature and morals.
3. Literature and morals.   4. Didactic literature—
History and criticism.   5. Aphorisms and apothegms—
History and criticism.   6. American literature—
History and criticism.   7. Literature, Comparative—
French and American.   8. Literature, Comparative—
American and French.   I. Title.
PQ145.1.E83H86   1987   810'.9'353   86-12570

ISBN 0-19-504180-1

2 4 6 8 10 9 7 5 3 1

Printed in the United States of America
on acid-free paper.

For
Douglas Armato
and
Christopher L. Miller

Preface

This book primarily addresses one question: Why do Americans—and American authors in particular—profess such moral sentiments while engaging so little in the traditionally moralistic literary genres of maxim and fable? My stance is that of an American who has spent a good deal of time studying the literature of my own country as well as that of France, where the properly moralistic genres flourished in the seventeenth and eighteenth centuries as nowhere else—but where, ironically, there has never been the sort of obsession with morality (in life and literature) that exists in America, which has produced such outbursts as the late John Gardner's *On Moral Fiction*.

The question is not one which may be answered by means of a linear, chronological comparison of the two literatures. My approach, instead, has been the only honest one which the subject will permit: to consider the various literary environments in both cultures, in which moral issues have arisen, progressing from one to the next in a sort of spiral development. Each chapter is a circle in the spiral, not pointing to the next so much as flowing into it. To begin with, there is the inevitable scrutiny of the history of the maxim in France and America. This is followed by a consideration of the fragment as theosophical meditation, and then as literary epistemology. The latter chapter is followed by a study of the role of the aphorism in deconstructionist criticism. The fable in both literary cultures comes into focus next. Finally, I am obliged to contemplate the survival of the maxim as a sort of negation of itself in modern poetry, both in the United States and in France. What emerges is not one answer to the question raised earlier but many, all of which I believe to be true and none of which is really as useful by itself as when considered with the others.

A note regarding references: I have dispensed with footnotes, incorporating parenthetical bibliographical references into the body of the text. Where but one work by a given author is cited throughout, only the author's name is provided, followed by the page number in question; if the author's identity is clear from the context, the page number will suffice. In cases where two or more works by the same author appear in the bibliography, each work is referred to in an abbreviated fashion. For instance, *Allegories of Reading* is abbreviated *A o R*, and "The Resistance to Theory" is abbreviated "R t T." A complete list of works cited appears at the end of this book. Translations are my own unless otherwise noted.

Baton Rouge, La.   J. H.
April 1986

Acknowledgments

Several parts of this book have been previously published in somewhat different form in the following journals, to whose editors I am grateful for permission to reprint: the first part of chapters 1 and 3 in *L'Esprit créateur* 22, no. 3 (Fall 1982) and 24, no. 3 (Fall 1984); chapter 2, in the *Massachusetts Review* 26, nos. 2–3 (Summer–Autumn 1985), and chapter 6 in the *South Atlantic Quarterly* 86, no. 1 (January 1987) (copyright © 1987 by Duke University Press).

I would also like to express my appreciation to the Council on Research of the Louisiana State University for its support of my work through the granting of two summer stipends, a partial stipend in 1983 and a full one in 1984. I am heavily indebted as well to the chairperson of my department, Nathaniel Wing, and to Henry L. Snyder, former dean of the College of Arts and Sciences at LSU, without whose active interest and support the present book might never have been finished. A special word of thanks is due to three friends and colleagues, Ross Chambers, Kate Cooper-Leupin and Alexandre Leupin, who read the manuscript and offered invaluable corrections and suggestions. The encouragement, intellectual stimulation, and friendship of my colleagues in the English Department at LSU—in particular James Olney, Lewis Simpson, and Gale Carrithers—have sustained me as well throughout the writing of this book.

Finally, I must express an immense debt to the staff of the Text Processing Center of the College of Arts and Sciences at LSU, without whose patient attention to detail the finished manuscript could not have appeared.

Contents

1 Introduction: The Golden Age of Aphorism   3
The Mad Judge, or Manners without Morals:
From La Rochefoucauld's *mot juste* to
Chamfort's *mot fou*
The World According to Poor Richard

2 Aphorism and Theology: Blaise Pascal,
Cotton Mather, Jonathan Edwards,
and the Sorcery of Rhetoric   26

3 Aphorism and Literary Epistemology:
Maurice Blanchot, Paul de Man, and
Marcel Proust   45

4 Aphorism and Criticism: Deconstruction and
the Commonplace Tradition   56

5 Aphorism and Fable: La Fontaine and
Joel Chandler Harris   75

6 Aphorism and Modern Poetry: The Advent
of the Antimaxim   91

7 Afterword   105

Works Cited   107

Index   111

THE PURITAN AND THE CYNIC

1

Introduction:
The Golden Age of Aphorism

The Mad Judge, or Manners without Morals:
From La Rochefoucauld's *mot juste*
to Chamfort's *mot fou*

The French word *maxime* comes from the Latin superlative of *magnus*, "great, large," as particularly applied to another Latin word, *sententia*, "opinion, thought," especially in the sense of judgment, a formally rendered decision. Hence the genre conceives itself etymologically as an *arrêt* or judgment of the highest, grandest order—a decision at once legal and literary. Embedded in the concept of such a genre is the same concern which faces any notion of legality: the question of whether law is based on a universal, immutable truth, or merely on the *sententiae* (ways of thinking, opinions) of its author or authors. Does law reflect opinion, or the natural law of immanent and perennial justice, as the eighteenth century and most notably John Locke conceived it? Laws have always existed as a social scaffolding, to order the relations of men in societies. We might conclude, then, that the maxim must represent the literary analogue of a law, both reflecting and enforcing the parameters of polite discourse and behavior. The problem confronted by the writer of maxims is much like the judge's, but with one essential difference: The writer has no written legal code to interpret, but rather his own observations.

This difference underlines the ambiguity of any judge's situation, be it literary or legal. According to the genealogy of the genre, the

3

business of the writer of maxims is to draft the truth into a literary code of law. There is no problem so long as "way of thinking, opinion," and "truth" are presumed to be synonymous, and the writer does not seriously question his role as a guide for the proper comportment of men in societies—so long as *maxima* continues to mean "greatest" in the sense of "universal." But what is the result when that premise is questioned, when the greatest way of thinking is also the most individual, when truth is seen as relative rather than universal, idiosyncratic instead of immanent?

Before attempting an answer, we ought to consider another assumption on which the genre of the maxim is based, the idea that the greatest and grandest truth is to be discovered in the minutest of observations. If truth is universal and intrinsic, it cannot depend on variables of scale. But as soon as the universal and the particular are not assumed to be synonymous, we enter the realm of relativism, and the very notion of truth is rendered problematic. Simply to observe that the truth on one scale is different from the truth on another is sufficient to introduce this problem. When *moeurs* and *morales* are no longer seen as coincident, each reflected in and by the other—when the physiognomy of men and their society is no longer thought to represent, in the classical tradition of Plato, Aristotle, Theophrastus, and Erasmus, the highest and only truth— then the writer of maxims must deal with a problem which no real judge ever confronts (see Brody and Van Delft). He must justify himself by redefining truth as a function of *morales,* of *moeurs,* of language, or of the writer himself.

The history of the genre in France may be read in this way as a progression from La Rochefoucauld's concept of morality as a legalistic code for promoting the appearance of virtue in society, a purely aesthetic virtue, toward a more radical consciousness of what is implied by this aestheticism. The effect of La Rochefoucauld's work is to obliterate any notion of a truth prior to appearance, any notion of a universality reflected in small details, in favor of a morality in which truth and virtue are realized by nothing but the effective illusion, artifice, and mise en scène of the same, and naturalness is defined as supreme paradox, the perfect success of artifice. There is no truth save in pleasing appearances, which is very close to saying that there is no truth, but only pleasing illusions of it. La Bruyère looks at La Rochefoucauld's aestheticism and finds it neither virtuous nor credibly natural nor pleasing in appearance, but rather grotesquely hypocritical. What he sees is an inevitable discontinuity of appearances, however well manipulated, the hypocrisy of a society which prefers the mask of virtue to the fact, the face, the substantial truth of merit. Because they are fragmentary and discontinuous, manners and appearances can only travesty virtue, conceal merit. La Rochefoucauld has taken away any universality of virtue, the immanence of truth; La Bruyère denies the integrity of appearances, manners, as its substitute.

If La Bruyère makes any effort to totalize truth, it is as merit, but this is not where the power of his observation lies. It lies rather in the denial that manners can be totalized into an aesthetic surrogate for morality. Vauvenargues makes a new effort to reinvent the truth, this time as neither appearance nor merit but the self. Virtue for him consists in integrating the manner, appearance, and essence of the self. But can the self be totalized any more than abstract truth? Only if we forget La Rochefoucauld and La Bruyère and lend credence to the possibility of integrating or totalizing manners and morals, essence and appearance, visage and mask—a possibility which both writers expose as primitively naive. Following them, the work of Vauvenargues represents an anachronism, but a necessary one. It displaces the focal point of the epigrammatic genre from society (La Rochefoucauld), and from the individual in society (La Bruyère), who is imprisoned and repressed by it, onto the self as its own society—a narrowing of scope which is also traceable through the work of these three.

It is tempting to read La Rochefoucauld, and indeed every moralist after him, as Philip Lewis, Jean Starobinski, and Roland Barthes have done more or less consistently, as inventors and players of a linguistic game which makes no pretense to reflect any totalizable truth. The epigram can be reduced to a structural exigency of NOUN / COPULATIVE / NOUN, and La Rochefoucauld's aesthetic morality can be read as replacing the opposition good / evil by the *jeu* of a discourse of observation and manner (Lewis, 26–30; Starobinski). Yet La Rochefoucauld does not seek to substitute form for morality, but rather to make form into morality, without spurning the latter at all. The genre does, as Lewis says, by its nature embrace the metalingual (a significative code) and the poetic (the play of writing for its own sake); this makes it possible to read any maxim as an attempt to totalize or as a repudiation of totalization, a pure *jeu du discours*. It must nevertheless be noted that neither La Rochefoucauld nor La Bruyère nor Vauvenargues is willing to forego a claim on the Logos, however they define it, and in that sense the readings by Philip Lewis, Roland Barthes, and Jean Starobinski are all partial. Faced with a text which, as Lewis astutely observes, presents itself as an exposé of signs as signs, they choose to emphasize the exposé rather than the effort and will to totalize which it represents (Lewis, 176–77).

La Rochefoucauld's stance appears at the peak of its paradoxicality in the following pair of citations. On the one hand, the thoughts and perceptions of men are relative, almost random, and not subject to reason or morality. This is precisely due to the impossibility of integrating, totalizing the self. The perceiving subjectivity cannot attain objective phenomenality and subjectivity at the same time; to perceive itself at all, it must stand back and recognize itself as other, and thus cannot avoid a discontinuity with itself. Introspection casts the self into the flickering instability of nonintegrity, displaces and scatters it in and among its own reflections:

Quand il s'agit de nous, notre goût n'a plus cette justesse si nécessaire . . . tout ce qui a du rapport à nous nous paraît sous une autre figure. Personne ne voit des mêmes yeux ce qui le touche et ce qui ne le touche pas; notre goût n'est conduit alors que par la pente de l'amour-propre et de l'humeur, qui nous fournissent des vues nouvelles, et nous assujettissent à un nombre infini de changements et d'incertitudes; notre goût n'est plus à nous, nous n'en disposons plus, il change sans notre consentement, et les mêmes objets nous paraissent par tant de côtés différents que nous méconnaissons enfin ce que nous avons vu et ce que nous avons senti. (La Rochefoucauld, 203)

When it is a question of ourselves, our taste no longer has that precision which is so essential . . . everything connected with us appears to us in a different light. No one sees in the same way that which affects him personally and that which does not; our taste is thus governed only by our self-love and our disposition of the moment, which always furnish new perspectives, and subject us to an infinite number of uncertainties and changes; our taste is no longer ours, we do not control it, it changes without our consent, and the same objects appear to us in so many different lights that we end up confusing what we have seen with what we have felt.

Yet within this discontinuity, which keeps the self from recognizing its own perceptions, La Rochefoucauld clings to the psychic and physical determinisms of *l'amour-propre* and *l'humeur*. In this refusal to allow indeterminacy to obey its own law, that is, to be without a determinate cause, he reminds one of Freud.

On the one hand, La Rochefoucauld eloquently describes the self's nonintegrity, while on the other hand he insists on the primacy of an integrity based in appearances, a self which is natural, true, and proper but the purest representation of successful artifice. The contradiction implicit in such a view is so extreme that it appears a plausible strategy. The "true" self does not exist in any primal state but must be brought into being. Yet it cannot be shaped by imitation; no copy will suffice, but only an original—an original which does not preexist the copies, but is realized as artifice which avoids mimesis. As a textual analogy, we might say that the natural self is to the counterfeit self as allegory is to the mimesis of realism. The true self is an allegory of its own being.

> Chacun veut être un autre, et n'être plus ce qu'il est: ils cherchent une contenance hors d'eux-mêmes, et un autre esprit que le leur; ils prennent des tons et des manières au hasard; ils en font l'expérience sur eux, sans considérer que ce qui convient à quelques-uns ne convient pas à tout le monde, qu'il n'y a point de règle générale pour les tons et pour les menières, et qu'il n'y a point de bonnes copies.
> (La Rochefoucauld, 189)

> Each wishes to be another, and not to be what he is: they look for a countenance outside themselves, and a spirit other than their own; they adopt tones and manners at random; they try them out on themselves, without considering that what suits some may not suit everyone, that there is no general rule for tones and manners, and that there are no good copies.

La Rochefoucauld wishes to make this allegory into the original, the Logos, the truth, the nature whose absence has made it possible.

La Bruyère follows the Aristotelian tradition in locating a bedrock of truth in human foible and vice—unchanged, he says in his *Discours sur Théophraste,* since classical antiquity. Nor is he willing to admit any uncertainty in his own work as observer, chronicler, and writer. Human behavior is subject to immutable laws; there is a correct way of expressing these laws, and it is La Bruyère's way—

these are the assumptions which subtend all that La Bruyère has to say. The writing of a maxim is the mimesis of a thought that has a particular shape and substance. Written thought must render, must represent the shape and substance, which in their turn reflect the truth of human behavior as it is and has always been.

> Entre toutes les différentes expressions qui peuvent rendre une seule de nos pensées, il n'y en a qu'une qui soit la bonne. *On ne la rencontre pas toujours en parlant ou en écrivant; il est vrai néanmoins qu'elle existe, que tout ce qui ne l'est point est faible, et ne satisfait point un homme d'esprit qui veut se faire entendre.* (La Bruyère, 71)

> Among all the different expressions which may render one of our thoughts, only one is the right one. *One does not always encounter it in speaking or in writing; it is nevertheless true that it exists, that everything which falls short of it is weak, and does not satisfy a man of wit who wishes to make himself understood.*

Truth exists prior to its own expression and apart from it. La Bruyère believes in truth no less than La Rochefoucauld, but his view of it could scarcely be more different.

Vauvenargues criticizes both for their pessimism, which he implicitly explains by their failure to provide a tenable basis for the integration of the self: La Rochefoucauld wishes to console us with the illusion of integrity, while La Bruyère can offer no more than the bitter spectacle of discontinuity between merit and reward, the true self and society's misconstrual of it, or, to borrow Bergson's terminology, the deep self and the social self. Vauvenargues would fill this gap by substituting *l'amour-pour-soi* for *l'amour-propre*. The distinction is based on little more than the wish that there be one, and that *l'amour-pour-soi* allow for altruism. Vauvenargues disputes both his predecessors. He believes in the primacy of a natural and passionate, true self which is by its nature disposed to be virtuous, and believes as well that good does not depend upon the intellect. He makes of this innate virtue an end both to the discontinuity between the self and society as described by La Bruyère, and to the nonintegrity of the self as described by La Rochefoucauld. This can be accomplished, however, only by a paradox even more extreme than La Rochefoucauld's. He calls the self's contamination by otherness—its nonintegrity—an instance of virtue (altruism), and cites this as proof of the integrity of goodness within the self. The nonintegrity of the self bears witness to the integrity of the self's goodness. What we have here is more than a paradox: a self-contradicting tautology of the form, "X's existence proves that X does not exist."

> Avec l'amour de nous-mêmes, disent-ils, on peut chercher hors de soi son bonheur; on peut s'aimer hors de soi davantage que dans son existence propre; on n'est point à soi-même son unique objet. L'amour-propre, au contraire, subordonne tout à ses commodités et à son bien être; il est à lui-même son seul objet et sa seule fin. (Vauvenargues, 56)

> With the love of ourselves, they say, one may seek one's happiness outside oneself; one may love oneself outside oneself more than in one's own existence; one is not one's own unique object. The love of self, on the contrary, subordinates everything to its convenience and its well-being; it is its own only object and end.

With *l'amour-propre* the self attempts its own totalization, tries to be its own object, and fails. In its recognition of itself as other in the other, in realizing its own discontinuity, says Vauvenargues, the self bears witness to a Logos, a truth, which is virtue, *l'amour-de-soi*. The existence of virtue, proved by the self's inability to totalize itself, totalizes Vauvenargues's moral system. This is how he attempts to resolve the incongruence of *moeurs* and *morales* made apparent by La Rochefoucauld and railed against by La Bruyère— incongruence which, since La Rochefoucauld, appears to have generated more and more radically paradoxical solutions.

Looking forward to Hegel's model of perception, Vauvenargues describes the self as recognizing itself as other in the other, and recognizing the other as itself in itself, in its own image. The surprisingly radical aspect of Vauvenargues's thought is in wishing to construct a moral system out of the self's insufficiency, its nonintegrity—*l'insuffisance de notre être*. (Vauvenargues, 57). Vauvenargues's work represents an honest attempt not just to have morality without totalization, moral manners without truth, which both his predecessors attempted more or less without realizing it, but consciously and deliberately to describe the self's *insuffisance,* to admit the impossibility of an objective subjectivity, and to call this instability virtue. The sheer intellectual pluck behind such an effort commands respect.

It is at this juncture in the historical dialectic of the genre that the work of Sébastien Roch Nicolas Chamfort occurs. If Vauvenargues's work is upliftingly and at times naively intrepid, Chamfort's is a stunning bolt, at once lugubrious and brazen. It begins by disparaging its own purposes, audience, and predecessors. Maxims, he tells his reader in his very first one, are for lazy and mediocre minds (Chamfort, 51). The mediocre reader, furthermore, ascribes a generality—truth, if you will—to the genre, to which none but a mediocre author would lay claim. Having gratuitously insulted us, he goes on to do the same to his predecessors, reducing them all to two fundamental fallacies: seeing human nature as evil and seeing it as good. In fact it is neither, or as he puts it, "*Est in medio verum*"(Chamfort, 54). Truth is in neither good nor evil but somewhere between them, in the middle distance. What can be between them but their mutual contamination, the involvement of each with the other? Neither is entirely itself, but exists only in relation to the other, defined as what the other is not. Neither can be the basis for a moral system because neither can be totalized, neither can be thought to think itself independently of the other. Hence the perfect uselessness of every moral work. There is no good or evil for the moralist to discover, much less impart. Consequently, his work has no impact or purpose in the world whatever, even among those lazy and mediocre enough to let themselves become "dupes of the charlatanry of moralists." (Chamfort, 119). The truth of Chamfort's moral universe (I use "moral" ironically, as he does) is neither here nor there but somewhere in between the things we know, the things to which we can give names such as "good" and "evil": it is not located in a particular conviction or observation, but rather in the discontinuity between any two opposites we might care to posit. The moralist may "aspire to virtue, but not to truth," for the only truth is the impossibility of a conclusion, of totalizing—the absence of truth.

In that case, what could virtue possibly be? Virtue, he says, would consist of "unifying opposites," of living in conformity with all the paradoxical exigencies of this truth. Thus virtue means totalizing the untotalizable, obliterating the space of discontinuity and difference across which good and evil flicker, reel, and flounder in mutual contamination, neither one being entirely itself. So real virtue is no more practicable than truth. Practical virtue consists in the acknowledgment and knowledge of truth as virtual rather than actual, self-contradictory by nature. "Dans les choses, tout est *affaires mêlées;* dans les hommes, tout est *pièces de rapport.* Au moral et au physique, tout est mixte. Rien n'est un, rien n'est pur" (Chamfort, 77). ("In things, all is *mixture;* in men, all is *connected pieces.* In the moral and the physical, everything is mixed. Nothing is whole, nothing is pure.") Books, including the works of moralists, cannot effect any good in the world, no matter how well conceived, written, or meant, no matter how seriously taken. To live, to observe, to write, no matter how well, is to be caught up in the play of discontinuity, decomposition, corruption, impurity, to be reminded of the radical alterity of truth and virtue.

> Ce serait une chose curieuse qu'un livre qui indiquerait toutes les idées corruptrices de l'esprit humain, de la société, de la morale, et qui se trouvent développées ou supposées dans les écrits les plus célèbres, dans les auteurs les plus consacrés; . . . On verrait que presque tous les livres sont des corrupteurs, que les meilleurs font presque autant de mal que de bien. (Chamfort, 52)
>
> A curious thing indeed would be a book which indicated all the corrupting ideas of the human mind, of society, of morality, which are developed or supposed in the most famous writings, in the most consecrated authors; . . . One would see that almost all books corrupt, and that the best do almost as much harm as good.

Practical virtue consists in the recognition of corruption, contamination, everywhere. The man who looks to reason to save him is "like a sick man poisoned by his doctor." If the physical world was begun by a benevolent deity, he must have left it to a bumbling one to finish the job; the moral world is no more than "the product of the whims of a devil gone mad" (Chamfort, 61, 62). Nothing is what it claims or seems to be, including this practical virtue. To live in perpetual awareness of the virtuality and paradoxicality of one's own pretenses, designs, aspirations, machinations, is to forgo all possibility of conventional contentment. There are, says Chamfort, only two ways to achieve any happiness. The first and more common way is by a "willful paralysis of the soul" (Chamfort, 77). This is the bliss of laziness and mediocrity. The result of the other way bears no resemblance to what is usually conceived as happiness, and is to be achieved only by wholly purging oneself of hope.

> L'espérance n'est qu'un charlatan qui nous trompe sans cesse; et,
> pour moi, le bonheur n'a commencé que lorsque je l'ai eu perdue.
> Je mettrais volontiers sur la porte du paradis le vers que le Dante a
> mis sur celle de l'Enfer: *Lasciate ogni Speranza, voi ch'entrate.*
> (Chamfort, 71–72)
>
> Hope is nothing but a charlatan who dupes us without cease; and for
> me happiness has begun only when I have lost hope. I would happily
> place on the door to paradise the verse which Dante placed on that
> of Hell: *Abandon all hope, you who enter here.*

It is by trying to look beyond the corruption, to an impossible conclusion, hoping for an end to it, that we make our virtuality un-
bearable. To live comfortably within it, we have to forgo the desire
to conclude. Nor does reason offer a third possibility of happiness.
The man who would have reason lead him to contentment is like
the one who has his mattress cleaned so often that he wears it out
and winds up having to sleep on the floor: He who submits all pleasure to analysis ends up without any (Chamfort, 84).

Because every aspect of our daily lives is paradoxical and virtual,
we live shrouded in illusions. Practical virtue consists in not trying
to put them off, which would be impossible, but in recognizing
them as illusions. Life, the disease for which sleep is a palliative
and death the only cure, is this play of illusoriness, this reading of
masks, the moralist's perspective on men and events as theatrical,
as masks (see Van Delft). The genealogy of the genre includes the
medieval Church's belief in the events of this life as representations, rehearsals of the higher life of the soul (Huizinga, 151–77).
La Rochefoucauld cast doubt on the spiritual level, the Logos of
such a system, but tried to reinvent a morality that could do without
it. All his successors in the French tradition accepted this premise,
but all until Chamfort struggled to put something on the empty throne
of Truth. Chamfort, however, is not interested in truth and says so.
He has turned the old notion of the moralist as interpreter and critic
of the human spiritual drama on its head. The moralist chases after
the masks in the drama as avidly as if he believed that there were
faces behind them, but does not turn away when the masks reveal
themselves as concealing—signifying—nothing.

> Il y a des hommes à qui les illusions sur les choses qui les intéressent
> sont aussi nécessaires que la vie. Quelquefois cependant ils ont des
> aperçus qui feraient croire qu'ils sont près de la vérité; mais ils s'en

éloignent bien vite, et ressemblent aux enfants qui courent après un masque, et qui s'enfuient si le masque vient à se retourner. (Chamfort, 120)

There are men for whom illusions concerning everything that interests them are as essential as life. Sometimes, however, they may have insights which would make one think they were close to the truth; but they quickly run from it, and are like children who run after a mask, and run away if the mask turns toward them.

Attainment of truth means the loss of illusion, and that is equated by Chamfort with the death of the soul: "la perte des illusions amène la mort de l'âme, c'est-à-dire un désintéressement complet sur tout ce qui touche et occupe les autres hommes (n'est-ce pas?)" (Chamfort, 57). ("The loss of illusions leads to the death of the soul, that is to say, to a complete disinterestedness regarding everything which affects and occupies other men [isn't this true?].") The death of the soul is disinterestedness, an indifference to the doings of other men which comes with the realization that there is nothing behind the masks. Those who have not perceived the death of the soul, to whom illusion is too necessary to be seen as illusion, who believe in a truth short of death, will hide their faces or take refuge within masks of their own, when the masks they have been pursuing fall away to reveal nothing except perhaps more masks. The pursuit of these masks is a game of boxes within boxes; there is always another box within the one we have just opened, the one we see. There is nothing to win, nothing in the boxes but other boxes—no soul, no Logos, no transcendental signified.

This death of the soul is not an event or a thing, but an emptiness, an absence which precedes our perception of it. Death is not totalization within the system of signifiers, or masks, but the end of wishing to totalize. It is not the end of life, but that which entirely exceeds the disease of life, its absolute other, the other of life-as-dying. It is the unqualifiable alterity of this mediated existence, death as death, rather than death as life, death-as-dying-as-life. This—the goal of all philosophy—is to be apprehended by the living, from within this sanitarium of life, only by indifference, as that which is not in any of the boxes we open in the game of perception, interpretation, communication. It is what we do not and cannot say. This disinterestedness is virtual, of course, and can be approached only asymptotically. For life, the disease, is interest. Life is a kind of

madness which cannot help attaching irrational significances, interpretations, souls to the masks that confront us. The only completely
disinterested subject is a dead one. The disease, the madness of
imagining faces where there are only masks, is the madness of im-
puting life, reality, a signified to a text, suspending disbelief, disinterestedness, and sanity long enough to believe in the illusion of
words, to allow the imagination to conjure images of reality from
a series of verbal masks.

In this sense, everyone is reading all the time. For Chamfort the
virtuous man, the moral man, is the one who tries not to forget that
he is mad, diseased, chasing a mask with no face behind it, writing
virtuous books which can only corrupt because they depend on the
very madness they attempt to surmount; without that madness they
could never be read or written. The reader, in his purest state of
delusion, is like the lover who has made up the object of his passion
out of his own need to be loved, out of the insanity which is his
own being, projecting his own fantasy behind the mask, the epi-
dermis, of the beloved:

> L'amour, tel qu'il existe dans la société, n'est que l'échange de deux
> fantaisies et le contact de deux épidermes. (Chamfort, 133)
>
> Love, as it exists in society, is nothing but the exchange of two
> fantasies and the contact of two epidermises.

> Il semble que l'amour ne cherche pas les perfections réelles; on dirait
> qu'il les craint. Il n'aime que celles qu'il crée, qu'il suppose; il res-
> semble à ces rois qui ne reconnaissent de grandeurs que celles qu'ils
> ont faites. (Chamfort, 136)
>
> It seems that love does not seek real perfections; one would rather
> say that it fears them. It loves only the perfections it creates, which
> it supposes; it resembles those kings who acknowledge only the
> greatnesses which they have created.

> On dit communément: "La plus belle femme du monde ne peut don-
> ner que ce qu'elle a; ce qui est très faux: elle donne précisément ce
> qu'on croit recevoir, puisqu'en ce genre c'est l'imagination qui fait
> le prix de ce qu'on reçoit. (Chamfort, 136; see also maxims 391 and
> 401, pp. 137, 139)
>
> It is commonly said: "The most beautiful woman in the world can
> give only what she has"; which is quite false: she gives precisely
> what one believes oneself to be getting from her, since in this genre
> it is the imagination which establishes the price of what one receives.

But if the lover, like the simple-minded reader, unaware of his own suspension of disbelief, seems ridiculous, it is only as a somewhat more feverish, delirious victim of the same infection. Love is more fun than marriage, says Chamfort, in the same way that novels are more fun to read than history (Chamfort, 137). The conventions governing the latter are more confining, more sober, but both are texts. The difference is merely one of conventions which govern composition and interpretation. Similarly, the man in love is like a reader of fairy tales, while the "reasonable" (perhaps married) man is like a reader of history (Chamfort, 140). Both are readers, and history, for being more credible, is no less a text, a mask, an illusion, than the fairy tale. The lover and the reader of fairy tales merit attention, because they are caricatures of the reasonable man and the reader of history. The latter, insofar as they believe their illusions, are even more ridiculous for being less obvious. The reasonable man's sensibility may be less distorting, less inflamed than the lover's, but it works by the same principle. The difference is one of convention and intensity. The following *pensée,* for instance, might appear to apply only to the lover.

> Toutes les fois que je vois de l'engouement dans une femme, ou même dans un homme, je commence à me défier de sa sensibilité. Cette règle ne m'a jamais trompé. (Chamfort, 131)
>
> Every time I see infatuation in a woman, or even in a man, I begin to mistrust his or her sensibility. This rule has never misled me.

Yet there is not for one moment a man or woman entirely free of some kind of infatuation. Stripped of all others, there would still remain the infatuation with self that is the basis for life. The reader of history is still a reader. If some sensibilities are more suspect than others, all are suspect.

Chamfort wrote in his *Eloge de Molière* that the comedy of character was no longer possible, for character, as theatrically understood, was no longer possible: "les caractères ont été détruits par l'abus de la société poussée à l'excès" (32). The precept of conformity had replaced character with mask, turned the theater of society into a mere masked ball in which everyone wears more or less the same disguise. The change is not in the masks themselves—not that they have supplanted any sort of authentic visage; rather, the masks have become homogeneous, indistinguishable from one another, so that it is no longer possible for the illusion of authenticity, of La Rochefoucauld's *honnêteté,* to take place. Now, says Chamfort, it is all too apparent that the observer of society faces masks rather than characters. This is no grist for the dramatist's mill, but rather for the moralist's.

But not for the moralist who would find truth or character behind or among the masks—such naive philosophers reminded Chamfort of African natives scouring the bushes for souls.

> J'ai lu, dans je ne sais quel voyageur, que certains sauvages de l'Afrique croient à l'immortalité de l'âme. Sans prétendre expliquer ce qu'elle devient, ils la croient errante, après la mort, dans les broussailles qui environnent leurs bourgades, et la cherchent plusieurs matinées de suite. Ne la trouvant pas, ils abandonnent cette recherche, et n'y pensent plus. C'est à peu près ce que nos philosophes ont fait, et avaient de meilleur à faire. (Chamfort, 56)

> I have read in some traveler or other that certain savages in Africa believe in the immortality of the soul. Without claiming to explain what becomes of it, they think it wanders, after death, in the bushes around their villages, and they look for it several mornings in a row. Not finding it, they abandon the search and think no more about it. This is just about what our philosophers have done, and they had much better things to do.

The moralist, as Chamfort understands him, does not search for anything. He neither wishes nor expects to turn up any valuable quarry during his forays into the societal bushes. He watches others, the searchers and the lookers, the savages, and reflects their striving and their obliviousness as passively as a mirror. He sheds his observations, his reflections of them, like a snake in perpetual molt, having no body to which the words might adhere, no Logos to give them closure. Chamfort, as Poulet has written, finds a duration of renewal in a constantly reenacted refusal of the present, a perpetual annihilation of present and self, a repeated self-execution. Thus what appealed to him about the French Revolution was its destructive potential, not its promise of progress. The moral stance is one of violent passivity.

> M. . . . disait qu'il fallait qu'un philosophe commençât par avoir le bonheur des morts, celui de ne pas souffrir et d'être tranquille; puis celui des vivants, de penser, sentir, et s'amuser. (Chamfort, 279)

> Mr. . . . used to say that a philosopher began by having the hap-
> piness of the dead, that of not suffering and of being at peace; then
> that of the living, of thinking, feeling, and amusing oneself.

This strategy relies on a consciousness of death as process, a pro-
gressive and constant degeneration which denies any integrity, any
character, to self and society, and which acknowledges that death-
as-process is not the end of philosophy, the purest and most passive
independence and refusal of time, death itself, but rather life. Thus
the moralist is like the dying man who, in order to avoid receiving
the sacraments, adopts the strategy of "pretending not to die."
(Chamfort, 324). His work is a lie against death, which it nevertheless looks to, reflects, and is. As life consists in pretending not
to die, writing maxims consists in pretending not to lie, pretending
that there is a truth where there is none, that there are faces where
there are only masks, that there is life where there is only death.
And yet, virtue consists in the self-knowledge of the pretense, in
not believing one's own lies and not pretending to believe them.

So it is that, with Chamfort, the maxim becomes a game of language played for its own sake, the poetic taking precedence over
the referential and the metalingual. It is he who first exploited those
qualities, innate in the genre, which Starobinski and Lewis somewhat misleadingly discover in his predecessor, La Rochefoucauld.
It is in Chamfort that the moralist gives up all of the judge's claim
to authority, to being a duly constituted interpreter of the law—all,
indeed, but the judge's mask. So he becomes something like the
lunatic on the streetcorner who claims to be a judge but knows he
is not, declaiming to mostly heedless, occasionally frightened pas-
sers-by on the uselessness of his and their own endeavors.

The World According to Poor Richard

The maxim has had only one significant practitioner in the history
of American letters: Franklin's "Poor Richard" Saunders. As Poor
Richard, Franklin did not compose maxims of his own so much as
recast and refine what others had written, freely plundering contemporary anthologies of the genre as did other printers of the day. His
goal in so doing was not at all literary renown but profit.

> Almanacs were a printer's gold mine: Hardly a household in the colonies was without one and often it was the only reading matter . . .
> Amid a wealth of astronomical, astrological, and meteorological information were sprinkled epigrammatic verses and improving aphorisms: "moral Sentences, prudent Maxims, and wise Sayings." Franklin changed the conventional format little but transformed the sayings, culled from the same anthologies as his competitors', into such nuggets of homely directness that Poor Richard became second only to the Bible as a source of proverbial wisdom. A rather grim wisdom it was, based on thrift, caution, an obsessive hankering for self-sufficiency. Countless school children have been nurtured on such maxims as "God helps them that help themselves," "For want of a Nail the Shoe was lost," or "The sleeping Fox catches no Poultry," indoctrinated whether they knew it or not with all the virtues that "make Fortune yield." A recipe for getting ahead, yes, laced even with a touch of irony, a joke or two inserted deliberately "since perhaps for their Sake light, airy Minds peruse the rest." But there is little joy in Poor Richard, no expansive generosity, no room for the carefree, unpremeditated spirit. (Lopez and Herbert, 38–39)

In fact, the proportion of Richard's maxims dealing with money is relatively small, but it is for them that the almanacs, and Franklin as a writer of maxims, are remembered. It is those particular maxims, many of which were collected in Richard Saunders' most popular work, *The Way to Wealth,* that elicited the most enthusiastic response in the American mind of the day.

Franklin made his living as a printer and a popular writer. The method by which he had learned to write well anticipates Poor Richard's practice as the American La Rochefoucauld: Meeting "with an odd volume of The Spectator," Franklin "thought the writing excellent and wished if possible to imitate it."

> With this view I took some of the papers, and, making short hints of the sentiment in each sentence, laid them by a few days, and then, without looking at the book, try'd to compleat the papers again, by expressing each hinted sentiment at length, and as fully as it had been expressed before, in any suitable words that should come to hand. Then I compared my Spectator with the original, discovered some of my faults, and corrected them. But I found I wanted a stock of words, or a readiness in recollecting and using them, which I thought I should have acquired before that time if I had gone on making verses; since the continual occasion for words of the same

import, but of different length, to suit the measure, or of different sound for the rhyme, would have laid me under a constant necessity of searching for variety, and have tended to fix that variety in my mind, and make me master of it. Therefore I took some of the tales and turned them into verse; and after a time, when I had pretty well forgotten the prose, turned them back again. I also sometimes jumbled my collections of hints into confusion, and after some weeks endeavored to reduce them into the best order, before I began to form the full sentences and compleat the paper. This was to teach me method in the arrangement of thoughts. (*Autobiography,* 19)

The passage is significant because it exposes Franklin's pragmatism. He shared with the French writers of maxims a preoccupation with style, with literary manners, but he did not arrive at such an attitude by exhausting the possibilities of a morality within manners, and so he never used his manners, his style, to represent that exhaustion of truth as the French did. Franklin could not have been less interested in the epistemological obstacles to representing the Good. This is not to say that he did not believe in the congruence of truth and form, but rather that he never became sufficiently aware of the problem to be concerned about it. It would be more accurate, though, to say that he assumed such a congruence rather than that he actively believed in it. Style as a reflection of truth was not what mattered; making money was. Good style was important because to Franklin the printer it was a commodity. It sold books. This meant that good style was defined much as the American literary canon (Strunk and White) defines it still—simple, easy of consumption, and accessible to as great an audience as possible, but not to an audience defined by noble status, wealth, a great deal of leisure time, and an overwhelming metaphysical and literary self-consciousness. Poor Richard Saunders declares frankly his reason for undertaking to write an almanac: "The Printer has offer'd me some considerable share of the Profits."

The plain Truth of the Matter is, I am excessive poor, and my Wife, good Woman, is, I tell her, excessive proud; she cannot bear, she says, to sit spinning in her Shift of Tow, while I do nothing but gaze at the Stars; and has threatned more than once to burn all my Books and Rattling-Traps (as she calls my Instruments) if I do not make some profitable Use of them for the good of my Family. (*Papers,* I, 311)

Thus the truth is not so much in words as in money, and only in words to the extent that they make money.

Of course, as already mentioned, Poor Richard is remembered for nothing so much as his contributions to the popular wisdom concerning money. "The Art of getting Riches," he wrote, "consists very much in Thrift" (*Autobiography*, 208). Words make money, in this case, by reinforcing an early and cherished tenet of bourgeois morality: that it ought not to be spent except on making more. This, one supposes, is what justifies spending money on an almanac: that it tells how to make more. Money becomes a material metonymy for moral uprightness and must be retained and increased. A loose pocketbook connotes loose morals.

> 1. When you incline to have new clothes, look first well over the old ones, and see if you cannot shift with them another year, either by scouring, mending, or even patching if necessary. Remember, a patch on your coat, and money in your pocket, is better and more creditable, than a writ on your back, and no money to take it off.
> 2. When you incline to buy China ware, Chinces, India silks, or any other of their flimsy, slight manufactures, I would not be so hard with you, as to insist on your absolutely resolving against it; all I advise is, to put it off (as you do your repentance) till another year, and this, in some respects, may prevent an occasion for repentance. (*Autobiography*, 211)

Franklin / Saunders tells his readers that they can make money and keep it by following his advice, so the purchase of the almanac is a highly moral act. Literature, and in fact morality too, are pragmatically subordinated to a principle of wealth. Neither the literature nor the morality, the manners nor the morals, the *forme* nor the *fond,* can be allowed to question its own rhetoric, because this would make it less salable, more effete, less accessible to the buying public as well as less useful in the life of business and the business of life.

Franklin's most successful effort as Poor Richard, *The Way to Wealth,* first known as *Father Abraham's Speech,* may also be his most exemplary. In this text the apocryphal aphorist hears himself quoted at great length by an old man whom he stumbles on quite by chance.

> I stopt my Horse lately where a great Number of People were collected at a Vendue of Merchant Goods. The Hour of Sale not being

come, they were conversing on the Badness of the Times, and one
of the Company call'd to a plain clean old Man, with white Locks,
Pray, Father Abraham, what think you of the Times? Won't these
heavy Taxes quite ruin the Country? How shall we be ever able to
pay them? What would you advise us to?—Father Abraham stood
up, and reply'd. If you'd have my Advice, I'll give it you in short,
for a Word to the Wise is enough, and many Words won't fill a
bushel, as Poor Richard says. (*Papers,* VII, 340)

Father Abraham goes on in like fashion, quoting Poor Richard at
every turn for several pages. More interesting than anything he says
is Richard's conclusion.

Thus the old Gentleman ended his Harangue. The People heard it,
and approved the Doctrine, and immediately practised the contrary,
just as if it had been a common Sermon; for the Vendue opened,
and they began to buy extravagantly, notwithstanding all his Cau-
tions, and their own Fear of Taxes. I found the good Man had thoroughly studied my Almanacks, and digested all I had dropt on those
Topicks during the Course of Five-and-twenty Years. The frequent
Mention he made of me must have tired any one else, but my Vanity
was wonderfully delighted with it, though I am conscious that not a
tenth Part of the Wisdom was my own which he ascribed to me, but
rather the Gleanings I had made of the Sense of all Ages and Na-
tions. However, I resolved to be the better for the Echo of it; and
though I had at first determined to buy Stuff for a new Coat, I went
away resolved to wear my old One a little longer. Reader, if thou
wilt do the same, thy Profit will be as great as mine. I am, as ever,
Thine to serve thee. (*Papers,* VII, 350)

In this one paragraph the difference between Franklin and the
French aphorists appears with glaring salience. We have already
seen how the French maxim depends on an acute tension between
particularity and universality, a tension which must always install
a distance within the maxim between observation of detail and pre-
tention to truth, a distance which is always a potential source of
irony and in Chamfort is fully realized as such. This ironic distanc-
ing is not inscribed within Franklin's aphorisms, but rather between
them and their author, and between them and their readers.

Franklin first projects a fictive voice (Poor Richard) to be the
author of his maxims, and then has that persona deny his authority in two ways: first by deferring to the usurpation of another fictive
voice (Father Abraham), and then by admitting the purely mimetic,

therefore counterfeit, nature of his authorship, harking back to the way in which Franklin had taught himself to write marketable prose. This irony is reflected, repeated, in the response of Father Abraham's listeners to his advice, a response which Richard represents as normal and even predictable. The pleasure which these consumers find in aphoristic discourse has very little to do with acting upon the truth it pretends to adumbrate, or with believing in such a truth. What sort of pleasure can it be, then, if not the linguistic sort which is at the heart of the French practice of the maxim as a literary genre? Such pleasure is achieved through irony, through a distance of paradox within the fragmentary text, and yet the irony and the paradox of Franklin's aphorisms are repressed in the texts and exiled to an imaginary and ironic space between author and fictive persona, between fictive persona and mimetic reader, in the discrepancy between the readers' (listeners') pleasure in the aphoristic text and their flagrant disavowal of its content by their acts.

Poor Richard celebrates hearing his own words parroted (words which he admits are not his) by affecting momentarily, and against his first intention, to act as though he believed them. His last statement is in fact far more ironic than any overtly ironic formulation could be, because the subject of its irony is precisely whether or not it is ironic: "Reader, if thou wilt do the same, thy Profit will be as great as mine. I am, as ever, Thine to serve thee." Does this mean that the reader has as much to save as Poor Richard by not buying a new coat, or that, by acting as though one believed in the truth of one's own discourse, one may make as much money from it as Poor Richard? What is to serve the reader—the example of the aphorism's content, or the example of Poor Richard's successful sale of the example of the aphorism's content by enveloping it in a marketable style? This essential ambiguity between the reader's profit and the author's is the basis for the entire industry of self-help books today. The irony so evident in the maxims of the French is here displaced outside the aphorism to create a distance between author and text, reader and text, a distance mediated only by profit, and by a very ironic equation of the author's profit with the reader's. The linguistic play, the irony, on which the maxim must depend is transposed into a principle of profit, which was never a significant variable in the genre's history in France.

Poor Richard might thus be read as ancestor of the most consistently successful of all American genres: the self-help book. The almanac, in fact, is nothing if not a financial, psychological, and spiritual self-help book—Louis Ruykeyser, Dr. Joyce Brothers, and Norman Vincent Peale all in one. All three must share, as authors of popular books proclaiming new and useful truth, Richard's implicit equation of the individual and public good with financial emolument. The most cursory scrutiny of an ad for a popular book club in a women's magazine reveals innumerable descendants of Richard Saunders: *Every Woman's Legal Guide; Revlon's Art of Beauty; Weight Watchers' Fast and Fabulous Cookbook; The Family Medical Guide; How to Be Your Own Sex Therapist; How to Prosper in the Coming Bad Years; Dr. Lawrence Peter's Why Things Go Wrong, or The Peter Principle Revisited; Men, an Owner's Manual; ESO: How You and Your Lover Can Give Each Other Hours of Extended Sexual Orgasm; What Every Woman Ought to Know about Love and Marriage* (by Dr. Joyce Brothers); *Dr. Burns' Prescription for Happiness*—the list goes on at length. The preoccupations reflected—money, law, and sex—would seem to make the average American book buyer into the most unabashed and zealous materialist (therefore Marxist) imaginable.

The titles listed above give some idea both of what a different direction the genre of moralism has taken in America, and of what the difference between Franklin and Chamfort must have been in order for such evolution to occur. Since Franklin, the fragment in America has divorced itself entirely from any pretense of exploring or seeking metaphysical truth. It survives, however, as the huge industry of the self-help book and also as an obsession with trivia. Such volumes as the Wallaces' *Book of Lists* are a contemporary analogue of Richard Saunders' fragmentary wisdom which, because of the nature of the almanac as repository of useful information, often tended to degenerate even in the eighteenth century into mere fragmentary data. Witness, for instance, Poor Richard's versified listing of conditions necessary for a legal transfer of land to occur.

RULES OF LAW FIT TO BE OBSERVED IN PURCHASING

From an Old Book
First, see the Land which thou intend'st to buy
Within the Sellers title clear doth lie.
And that no Woman to it doth lay claim,

By Dowry, Jointure, or some other Name,
That it may cumber. Know if bound or free
The Tenure stand, and that from each Feoffee
It be released: That the Seller be so old
That he may lawful sell, thou lawful hold.
Have special Care that it not mortgag'd lie,
Nor be entailed on Posterity.
Then if it stand in Status bound or no:
Be well advised what Quit Rent out must go;
What Custom, Service hath been done of old,
By those who formerly the same did hold,
And if a wedded Woman put to Sale,
Deal not with her, unless she bring her Male,
For she doth under Covert-Baron go,
Altho' sometimes some also traffick so.
                              (*Autobiography,* 213–14)

Under the heading "Profitable Observations and Notes," we find such information as: "All Measures of Longitude are deduced from Barley corns: Three Barley corns make an Inch, 12 Inches a foot . . . in a Mile are . . . 190080 Barley corns" (*Papers,* 291). If Richard Saunders were alive today, he would doubtless include the same sort of aphoristic but hopelessly trivial observations (in the style of Ripley's "Believe It or Not") as these, all culled from the Wallaces' book:

A herring once lived to be 19 years old.

In a recent poll of human fears, twice as many people were afraid of speaking in public as they were of dying.

Making love uses up less calories than throwing a frisbee.

There is in all these clipped observations a deference to fact, to data, to the materially real, which never allows any doubt of the metaphysical grounding of such reality, which never accounts, for instance, for the subjectivity of data or the relativity of perception. This concern with fact ignores, then, the conclusions of Einstein and Heisenberg within the very realm of science, esteemed by pragmatic Americans as the only "real" realm of truth since Franklin's day (let us not forget that Franklin considered himself first and foremost a man of science, and is remembered first by every American schoolchild as flying a kite in a thunderstorm in order to experiment with electricity), not to mention the more pertinent doubts of Paul de Man, Jacques Derrida, and Michel Foucault. At the same time, the data cited above owe their punch to a certain wry, aphoristic pithiness which implies assumption of and allusion to a certain essence of bedrock truth. The truth implied would, however, have to be rather hopelessly, if not diabolically, banal, to infer from such trivial fragments as the following, which, like the ones cited above, are taken from the back jacket cover of the Wallaces' *Book of Lists:*

> Isaac Newton, Immanuel Kant, John Ruskin, all had one thing in common—they died virgins.
>
> King Henry VIII's second wife, Anne Boleyn, had three breasts— and wore long sleeves to hide her six fingers.

The trend since Franklin's day has obviously been away from the generalization of the maxim, its pretense to unite the universal and the fragmentary, and toward an obsession with the most recondite particularity. But the bizarrerie of detail charms because it seems to partake of a pattern of truth—truth as data, as matter, as palpably real, not metaphysical. It is here that the self-righteous and fire-breathing Marxist becomes identical with the most plumply self-satisfied bourgeois—which may explain why so many American critics, comfortably nestled all their lives in the bosom of American materialistic bourgeois culture, have sought refuge from de Man and Derrida in a reaction to bourgeois culture which calls itself Marxism but which in fact is nothing but a negative duplication of bourgeois materialism. The trend which Franklin began as a gleaner, rather than creator, of truth continues. The truth is not a matter of formulation. It exists; it needs only to be cast in a salable style and format. What Poor Richard defined as the essence of morality in the eighteenth century—health, wealth, and wisdom, with a liberal accent on the middle term—has been amended only slightly since the eighteenth century to include sexual well-being. This may explain why the aphorism as high literature could not be written in America until recently, when, because of a general failure of positive metaphysical truth, of truth as it had been understood before in the West, an antimaxim came into being (see chapter 6). In the meantime, serious moralistic discourse hid itself in other genres, from the corners and crevices of which, maximlike pronouncements grin and leer like gremlins. We shall see how and try to know why.

2

Aphorism and Theology:
Blaise Pascal, Cotton Mather, Jonathan Edwards, and The Sorcery of Rhetoric

The material world, and all things pertaining to it, is by the creator wholly subordinated to the spiritual and moral world.
> —JONATHAN EDWARDS, *Images or Shadows of Divine Things*

Chrysostom, I remember, mentions a *Twofold Book of* GOD; the Book of the *Creatures,* and the Book of the Scriptures: GOD having thought first of all as . . . by his *Works,* did it afterwards . . . by his *Words.* We will now for a while read the *Former* of these *Books,* 'twill help us in reading the *Latter:* They will remarkably assist one another.
> —COTTON MATHER, *The Christian Philosopher*

All the visible world is but an imperceptible trace in the ample bosom of nature.
> —BLAISE PASCAL, *Pensées*

It seems obvious that the Americans Mather and Edwards saw nature, as a text, rather differently from Pascal. Indeed, that they understood the subjectivity of perception quite differently: Instead of a dualism of subject and object, mediated imperfectly by the imperfect senses and intellect, Mather and Edwards saw a confirmation of Bunyan's view of the world as allegory. Subject and object were subsumed and united in the act of perception as they saw it, and perception was always, on an ultimate level, an apprehension of divine truth. Edwards, in espousing the scientific and philosophical advances of the seventeenth and early eighteenth centuries, distanced himself from the "allegorical fancy" of Mather. The discipline of science, as Edwards conceived it, was the only means of fusing perception and object, subject and object. Mather read nature in a more simply Bunyanesque fashion, using an allegorical imagination to uncover divine order. So much for their differences. Edwards' thought merely refines Mather's, bringing it more into accord with the new scientism. Both believed in the "science of typology," acording to which every event (type) in scripture referred to the ultimate event (antitype) of Christ's life and crucifixion. Both believed that typology applied not only to scripture but to the natural world and history. Their differences lie only in their manner of discovering and elaborating types. For them, typology had always opposed itself to tropology, or rhetoric, in an extremely telling way: The latter was heathen and agnostic play with figures without any regard for divine truth. The tegument binding subject and object, subject and subject, was for Mather and Edwards this ultimate truth of sacred revelation, whether perceived through science or allegory.

Because, however, of the subordination of the human, material world to the spiritual one, the mediation of spirit by matter, Puritan discourse—however wishfully positive and even dogmatic—is haunted by insecurity. That very uncertainty is the reason for Edwards' need for and appeal to science, and for Mather's redundant citation of nonpuritan authors to support puritan doctrine, ignoring or repressing any sense of the contradictions to which this exposed his own dogma. That insecurity, the hidden, unspeakable burden of puritan thought, would express itself most explicitly in the fear of witchcraft. The science of typology expresses hope whose desperation is apparent in the rather dogmatic fervency of its proponents. Typology wishes to suppose that there is a unity and a wholeness about human perception, the natural world, and language itself; that, in linguistic terms, there is an irreducible unity binding the parts of every sign—the word or letter, its meaning, and the object or idea referred to. Tropology, the classical art of rhetoric, was anathema because it introduced relativism. Using it, a speaker or writer could manipulate signs to his own particular, individual end, rather than the one absolute end of the Deity.

Pascal, on the other hand, found typology "precious," and condemned this will to epistemological integration as a primitive contradiction: It uses the means of classical rhetoric while refusing to acknowledge the absolute contradiction on which all tropes (types) must be based—irony, indirection, saying one thing and meaning another, a chain of substitutions of which the end, the final meaning, cannot be reached by mortal man. It is on this very contradiction that Pascal founds his concept of faith, in starkest contrast with the positivistic theology of the Puritans. He notes: "Deux erreurs. I. prendre tout littéralement. 2. prendre tout spirituellement" (34). ("Two errors: 1. to take everything literally. 2. to take everything figuratively.") And yet typology embraces both errors, as does Christian fundamentalism today, insisting that every word of scripture is true both literally and figuratively, as a type. Otherwise, it would have to be admitted that the letter is not true in every way, that there is a certain relativism in the very concept of truth. Pascal establishes religious sentiment on this breach within the letter, within perception, within truth, in a statement which Mather and Edwards could not have found other than popish and heretical:

> Car enfin qu'est-ce que l'homme dans la nature? Un néant à l'égard de l'infini, un tout à l'égard du néant, un milieu entre rien et tout, infiniment éloigné de comprendre les extrêmes; la fin des choses et leurs principes sont pour lui inviciblement cachés dans un secret impénétrable. (116)

> For finally, what is man within nature? A nothingness in relation to an infinity, an everything in relation to a nothingness, a mean between nothing and everything, infinitely far from comprehending the extremes; the end of things and their principles are for him invincibly hidden in an impenetrable secret.

The proof of God for Pascal is the ineluctable contradictoriness and impotence of human substance and thought, the fact that one may intimate the infinity of God only through the contingency of the letter or some other sign system, as for instance mathematics (Pascal was a mathematician). Man is an ironic paradox: "Nous sommes quelque chose et nous ne sommes pas tout" (118). ("We are something and yet we are not all.") Human thought cannot aspire beyond the irony and paradoxicality, the indirection of tropes, whether in language, science, or religion.

> Voilà notre état véritable. C'est ce qui nous rend incapables de savoir certainement et d'ignorer absolument. Nous voguons sur un milieu vaste, toujours incertains et flottants, poussés d'un bout vers l'autre;

quelque terme où nous pensions nous attacher et nous affermir, il
branle, et nous quitte, et si nous le suivons il échappe à nos prises,
nous glisse et fuit d'une fuite éternelle; rien ne s'arrête pour nous.
C'est l'état qui nous est naturel et toutefois le plus contraire à notre
inclination. Nous brûlons de désir de trouver une assiette ferme, et
une dernière base constante pour y édifier une tour qui s'élève à
[l']infini, mais tout notre fondement craque et la terre s'ouvre jus-
qu'aux abîmes.

Ne cherchons donc point d'assurance et de fermeté; notre raison
est toujours déçue par l'inconstance des apparences: rien ne peut fixer
le fini entre les deux infinis qui l'enferment et le fuient. (119)

There is our true state. It is what makes us incapable of knowing
with certainty and of not knowing with absoluteness. We float on a
vast middle space, always uncertain and wavering, pushed from one
end toward another; on whatever limit we think to attach and affirm
ourselves, it moves, and leaves us, and if we follow it, it slips from
our grasp, slides, and escapes in an eternal flight; nothing stops itself
for us. This is the state which is natural to us yet is the most contrary
to our wishes. We burn with the desire to find a firm seating, and
a final, constant basis on which to raise a tower rising to infinity,
but all our foundations crack and the earth opens to abysses.

Let us not, then, seek any assurance or firmness; our reason is
ever deceived by the inconstancy of appearances: nothing can fix the
finite between the two infinities which enclose it and escape it.

Pascal often expresses himself in aphoristic formulations, as above.
Such expressions turn on a tension, a paradox of individual expression or perception and common knowledge. If they are to succeed,
we must recognize them as true and yet acknowledge their originality. Like geometrical figures suspended in the mind, they occupy
a highly charged empty space of apposition, of mutually dependent
and contradictory propositions: "Quand on lit trop vite ou trop
doucement on n'entend rien" (54). ("When one reads too fast or
too slowly, one understands nothing.") A successful maxim cannot
be reduced to a "type."

In contrast with Pascal's aphoristic virtuosity is Cotton Mather's
truly bizarre circumspection with regard to the genre. He holds it
entirely at arm's length, embracing it no further than quotation will
permit, affirming its inevitability even as he refuses to enact it in
his own name. More peculiar still is the fact that he uses aphorisms
to explain and justify this self-contradictory stance.

In prosecuting this *Intention*, the Reader will continually find some *Author* or other *quoted*. This constant Method of *Quoting*, 'tis to be hoped, will not be censured, as proceeding from an *Ambition to intimate and boast a Learning*, which the *Messieurs du Port-Royal* have rebuked; and that the Humour for which *Austin* reproached *Julian*, will not be found in it: . . . "Who can hear this and not be frightened by the very sound of the names—provided he is not learned, as most men are not—and who but will consider you great because you know so much?" Nor will there be discernible any Spice of the impertinent Vanity, which *La Bruyère* hath so well satirized: "*Herillus* will always *cite*, whether he speaks or writes. He makes the *Prince of Philosophers* to say, *That Wine inebriates;* and the *Roman Orator, That Water temperates it*. If he talks of *Morality* it is not he, but the Divine *Plato*, who affirms, *That Virtue is amiable, and Vice odious*. The most common and trivial things, which he himself is able to think of, are ascribed by him to Latin and Greek Authors." But in these *Quotations*, there has been proposed, first a due *Gratitude* unto those, who have been my *Instructors;* and indeed, *something within me* would have led me to it, if *Pliny*, who is one of them, had not given me a Rule; . . . "It is noble to acknowledge by whom you have profited." It appears also but a piece of *Justice*, that the *Names* of those whom the Great GOD has distinguished, by employing them to make those *Discoveries*, which are here collected, should live and shine in every such Collection. (*Selections*, 288–89; I have given only translations of the Latin authors quoted.)

Mather cites the very adages which cast him in the worst light, which expose most nakedly the contradictions of his rhetoric. It is as though he wished to make a point of his own inconsistency, as though he were proud of it. But what one finds here is a difference of perspective. Mather himself refuses to enact the paradoxicality of aphoristic discourse. His relying on the aphorisms of others reflects a profound sense of the propriety of such texts, of their integration with authors and subjects. Mather's task is to enact the unity of author and aphorism, not the aphorism itself. For him, the chief property of the epigram is not paradox, not a suspension of subjectivity in the tension of two equally true and mutually exclusive observations, reflecting the suspension of the mind between greatness and smallness, in an abyss of rhetoric and relativity. Instead, Mather reads aphorisms as Edwards would read the new scientific advances: as perceptions which enact a unity of subject and object, author and text. Pascal bases his faith on a view of human subjectivity as an illusory, paradoxical, and unfathomable mystery. This is why he condemns the use of the first-person pronouns *I* and *me*. But Mather construes Pascal quite differently, as implying not that subjectivity is vain and ephemeral and that it is better to inscribe such evanescence forthrightly in one's own writing, but rather that the guarantor of thought's propriety and integrity is God, not the self.

> A considerable Body of Men (if the *Jansenists* may now be thought so) in *France*, have learnt of Monsieur *Pascal*, to denote themselves by the *French* Impersonal Particle *On;* and it was his opinion, that an honest Man should not be fond of *naming himself*, or using the word *I*, and *ME*, that *Christian Piety* will annihilate our I, and ME, and *Human Civility* will suppress it, and conceal it. (*Selections*, 289)

So also Edwards, for whom the antitype is the ur-text or Logos, with which every text, every observation "disciplined and guided by science," is integrated.

> Images of divine things. It is with many of these images as it was with the sacrifices of old: they are often repeated, whereas the antitype is continual and never comes to pass but once. Thus sleep is an image of death that is repeated every night; so the morning is the image of the resurrection; so the spring of the year is the image of the resurrection which is repeated every year. And so of many other things that might be mentioned, they are repeated often, but the antitype is but once. The shadows are often repeated to show t[w]o things, viz., [1] that the thing shadowed is not yet fulfilled and 2. to signify the great importance of the antitype that we need to be so renewedly and continually put in mind of it. (94–95)

In his *Images or Shadows of Divine Things,* Edwards does not use the same strategem as Mather to keep the aphorism "proper." He simply assumes that, in every natural phenomenon, there is a type to be discovered, and in every text worthy of the name, a truth derived from scripture. Here are two examples:

> The trial of gold and silver in the fire is a type of the trying of saints and their graces by persecution and other occasions of suffering and self-denial for God's sake, whereby the gold and silver is not only found to be pure, but is refined and purified more from dross and made much better. So those trials of the saints not only prove their

sincerity, but refines them, purges away their dross, strengthens their graces, and purges them from impure mixtures. (58)

There are three sorts of inhabitants of this world inhabiting its three regions, viz., the inhabitants of the earth, and the animals that inhabit the waters under the earth, and the fowls of heaven that inhabit the air or firmament of heaven. In these is some faint shadow of the three different sorts of inhabitants of the three worlds, viz., earth, heaven, and hell. The birds represent the inhabitants of heaven. These appear beautiful above the beasts and fishes; many of them are decked with glorious colours, whereas others do but go on the earth or move in the waters. These fly with wings and are above all kinds of animals, employ themselves in musick, many of them as it were sweetly praising their creator. The fishes in the waters under the earth represent the inhabitants of hell. The waters in Scripture is represented as the place of the dead, the Rephaim, the destroyers; and whales and sea monsters that swim in the great deep are used in Scripture as emblems of devils and the wrath of God, and the miseries of death and God's wrath are there compared to the sea, the deeps, to floods and billows and the like. (82–83)

Edwards virtually plagiarizes (paradoxically, given his and Mather's emphasis on the propriety of the text) Pascal's famous essay on the "Disproportion of Man," but with a very telling omission: He sees only one infinity where Pascal sees two. Man is not suspended between two unfathomables, but bound by spirit to one infinite Greatness.

That the earth is so small a thing in comparison of the distance between it and the highest heaven that, if we were there, not only the high palms and highest mountains would look low, whose height we gaze and wonder at now, but the whole earth would be less than nothing, nothing could be seen of it. Yea, if it were many million times bigger than it is, yea, probably many millions of millions times, it would still be less than nothing. It seems to typifie how that worldly things, all worldly honour and pleasure and profit, yea, the whole world and all worldly things put together, is so much lower and less than heavenly glory. Then when the saints come to be in heaven, all will appear as it were infinitely less than nothing. (57)

By excluding the infinity of smallness, Edwards avoids the irony, the negative force of apposition in Pascal's rhetoric. Thus Edwards never practices the kind of rigorous play with aphoristic paradox (rather like geometrical figures) so typical of Pascal. His fragment texts read more like exercises in analogy, and there is never any tension of surprise in them. They are simply sermonettes, depicting nature as an allegory of divine purpose.

What is most interesting about the "thoughts" of Mather and Edwards (the rough equivalent in their works of Pascal's *Pensées*) is that, by refusing to embrace the paradoxicality of aphorism, they do not escape it but merely repress it. Edwards parodies the very science which he claims as the tegument of his discourse (making birds out to represent angels, and whales, devils, without the slightest regard for their places in nature—a maneuver that is surprising despite the primitive state of zoology at the time). Mather, on the other hand, quotes aphorisms whose wisdom runs directly counter to his own citation of them. The way in which Mather dismisses readers who would not acknowledge his wisdom may offer a clue as to the reasons for his and Edwards' literary and epistemological differences with Pascal, and shed some light on the American literary mind of the time.

> Sure I am, Such *Essays* as these, to observe, and proclaim, and publish the *Praises* of the Glorious GOD, will be *desirable* and *acceptable* to all that have a *right Spirit* in them; *the rest,* who are *blinded,* are Fools, and unregardable: As little to be regarded as a *Monster* flourishing a *Broomstick*! (*Selections,* 290)

The only alternative to Mather's and Edwards' view of all signs, natural and linguistic, as anchored in and integrated with a Divine Logos, is the free play of causeless effects, which in Mather's writings is none other than witchcraft. One of the earliest definitions of *spell* is simply "to discourse . . .; to talk, converse or speak" (OED). The word is closely associated, in its etymological origins, with the *secular* practice of rhetoric. A magical spell, the sorcery which Mather spent many pages describing and condemning, is nothing but a causeless effect, the production of signs, phenomena, which are not integrated with the Antitype or Divine Logos, a disembodied voice, an invisible source.

> . . . as she [Phebe Chandler, a victim of witch magic] was at several times crossing the Fields, she heard a voice, that she took to be Martha Carriers, and it seem'd as if it was over her Head. The voice told her, she should within two or three days be Poisoned. Accordingly, within such a Little time, One Half of her Right Hand became

greatly swollen, and very painful; also a part of her Face; whereof she can give no account how it came. (*Narratives,* 243)

The devil is a hollow, void, counterfeit Logos; evil appears in all of Mather's writings on witchcraft as a denial of the wholeness of all natural phenomena, of the word in the service of the Deity, of scripture. Rhetoric, if it is not logocentric, deocentric, is magical, apparitional. A common talent ascribed to witches was the ability to appear far from their actual whereabouts, to be simultaneously in several places, and to metamorphose into many different shapes, animal as well as human. Witchcraft, then, is an abuse of nature's rhetoric.

John Louder testify'd, that upon some little controversy with Bishop [Bridget Bishop, accused of witchcraft] about her fowles, going well to Bed, he did awake in the Night by moonlight, and did see clearly the likeness of this woman grievously oppressing him; in which miserable condition she held him, unable to help him self, till near Day. He told Bishop of this; but she deny'd it, and threatned him very much. Quickly after this, being at home on a Lords day, with the doors shutt about him, he saw a Black Pig approach him; at which he going to kick, it vanished away. Immediately after, sitting down, he saw a Black thing Jump in at the Window, and come and stand before him. The Body was like that of a Monkey, the Feet like a Cocks, but the Face much like a mans. He being so extreemly affrighted, that he could not speak, this Monster spoke to him, and said, "I am a Messenger sent unto you, for I understand that you are in some Trouble of Mind, and if you will be ruled by me, you shall want for nothing in this world." Whereupon he endeavoured to clap his hands upon it; but he could feel no substance, and it jumped out of the window again; but immediately came in by the Porch, though the Doors were shut, and said, "You had better take my Counsel!" He then struck at it with a stick, but struck only the Groundsel, and broke the Stick. The Arm with which he struck was presently Disenabled, and it vanished away. He presently went out at the Back-Door, and spyed this Bishop, in her Orchard, going toward her House; but he had not power to set one foot forward unto her. Whereupon returning into the House, he was immediately accosted by the Monster he had seen before; which Goblin was now going to Fly at him; whereat he cry'd out, "The whole Armour of God be between me and you!" So it sprang back, and flew over the Apple Tree, shaking many Apples off the Tree, in its flying over. At its Leap, it flung Dirt with its Feet against the Stomach of the

Man; whereon he was then struck Dumb, and so continued for three
Days together. (*Narratives,* 226–27)

Note the way in which a scriptural aphorism is quoted against the
chimerical power of evil, just as Mather cites epigrams against the
breach in his own discourse. The witches are most often reported
as shapes without substance: "[Goodwife] Safford after this de-
clared herself to be afflicted by the Shape of [Elizabeth] How; and
from that Shape she endured many Miseries" (*Narratives,* 238).
"Witchcraft," wrote Mather, "seems to be the Skill of Applying the
Plastic Spirit of the World unto some unlawful purposes, by means
of a Confederacy with Evil Spirits" (*Narratives,* 246). Witchcraft
is precisely anything that defies understanding, anything that exceeds the economy of deocentric meaning.

Rhetoric, then, as Paul de Man defined it (after Nietzsche), is
nothing but witchcraft, and the same could be said of secular literature: "Rhetoric is a *text* in that it allows for two incompatible,
mutually self-destructive points of view, and therefore puts an insurmountable obstacle in the way of any reading or understanding"
(*A o R,* 131). This property of rhetoric is nowhere better exemplified than in Pascal's epigrammatic formulations. Any good maxim,
in fact, depends on such tension of self-contradiction, at once universal and contingent, fragmentary. Witchcraft, to Mather and indeed to the puritan mind, was none other than the residue of any
text which resists understanding—a residue that, in the view of de
Man and of Pascal as well (both in the French tradition), constitutes
the heart of any text, and also, for Pascal, the foundation of faith
(precisely the lack of any foundation at all).

There is no place in the puritan mind of Cotton Mather for any
such resistance to integration. He says so in dangerously and tell-
ingly aphoristic language: "Witchcraft will not be fully understood,
until the Day when there shall not be one Witch in the World"
(*Narratives,* 247). Translation: "That which cannot be understood
will not be understood until the day when there is nothing which
cannot be understood." This is yet another illustration of the way
in which aphoristic discourse may be avoided only at the cost of
having it burst the seams of one's sentences from within. Jonathan
Edwards, if less interestingly melodramatic in his meditations, conceives evil in much the same way, as a causeless effect, a spell, a

charm, an invisible and therefore inescapable snare: "The serpent's *charming* of birds and other animals into their mouths, and the spider's taking and sucking the blood of the fly in his snare are lively representations of the Devil's catching our souls by his temptations" (45; my emphasis).

There are two chief consequences of this puritan rhetoric. The first is obviously a tendency to project, objectify, and repress the darker, innately uncontrollable underside of rhetoric and knowledge—irony, paradox, nonintegrity. The second is the tendency of this epistemological undertow, though repressed, to twist, turn, and writhe inside the supposedly integrated pronouncements of anyone who would deny it. This paradoxicality, this treacherousness, appears in Pascal as the very means of his literary enterprise and thus its chief content as well. The Frenchman would embrace it freely, while the Americans somewhat comically attempt to deny it even as they enact it, rather like someone engaged in coitus while pretending to read a book. If we are to believe scholars such as Perry Miller and Sacvan Bercovitch, who argue that the puritan mind had a large measure of influence on what would become the American mind, we ought to see this same phenomenon repeat itself in later American literature. And indeed, we do.

What John T. Irwin, in his *American Hieroglyphics,* attributes to Champollion's discovery of the Rosetta stone—the American fascination with hieroglyphics in the early nineteenth century—has a great deal more to do with the heritage of this puritan rhetoric. Irwin traces the origin of American symbolism to the Egyptian hieroglyph. Yet in fact, American fascination with the hieroglyph makes much more sense in light of the rhetorical practice of Mather and Edwards. The symbol, like the hieroglyph, reflects a preoccupation with the pure figure, the pure trope, by which I mean a trope that absolutely resists integration with any particular meaning. A hieroglyph demands the invention of a code by which it may be deciphered, translated; consequently, it introduces the element of interpretation into reading and understanding. Henceforth there must be mediation between subject and object; the unity which Edwards (and Mather, in a more primitive way) read into subjectivity is revealed as an illusion. Such sleight-of-mind can be sustained only as long as the pure figure, the opaque sign, the causeless effect, is called evil and repressed. The pure trope transgresses the law of typology, divine integrity. By introducing the factor of interpretation, translation, it opens up the possibility of different interpretations, good translations and bad ones,. all approximative and imperfect, unintegrated with their object, the original. The original or object of understanding is revealed, in an ultimate perspective, as being ever absent, the illusion of its immediacy always having to be created by the mediation of interpretation.

This raises the disturbing possibility, within puritan rhetoric, that all literary practice is witchcraft. Nathaniel Hawthorne knew this very well, as for instance when he wrote "The Devil in Manuscript."

> "I do believe," said he, soberly, "or, at least, I would believe if I chose, that there is a devil in this pile of blotted papers . . ."
> "Have you felt nothing of the same influence?"
> "Nothing," replied I, "unless the spell be hid in a desire to turn novelist, after reading your delightful tales."
> "Novelist!" exclaimed Oberon, half seriously. "Then, indeed, my devil has his claw on you! You are gone! You cannot even pray for deliverance!" (*Tales,* 330–31)

Evil, sin itself, as transgression against the integration of holy order, is nothing but a pure trope, as in "Young Goodman Brown": "A basin was hollowed, naturally, in the rock. Did it contain water, reddened by the lurid light? or was it blood? or, perchance, a Liquid flame? Herein did the Shape of Evil dip his hand . . ." (*Tales,* 287). Brown dreams (or does he?) that he has witnessed, and almost participated in, a ritual of witchcraft. The effect on him of such a hieroglyph is that the integration of the Sacred Word, of any sign, is forever shaken. He cannot know for certain that he only dreamed the vision of the minister and all the citizens of the town as witches. In Goodman Brown the insecurity of puritan thought, its uncertain Calvinist underbelly, is exposed.

> Had Goodman Brown fallen asleep in the forest, and only dreamed a wild dream of a witch-meeting?
> Be it so, if you will. But alas! it was a dream of evil omen for young Goodman Brown. A stern, a sad, a darkly meditative, a distrustful, if not a desperate man, did he become, from the night of that fearful dream. On the Sabbath-day, when the congregation were singing a holy psalm, he could not listen, because an anthem of sin rushed loudly upon his ear, and drowned all the blessed strain. When

> the minister spoke from the pulpit, with power and fervid eloquence, and, with his hand on the open Bible, of the sacred truths of our religion, and of saint-like lives and trimphant deaths, and of future bliss or misery unutterable, then did Goodman Brown turn pale, dreading, lest the roof should thunder down upon the gray blasphemer and his hearers. (*Tales,* 288–89)

Young Goodman Brown merely pursues the logic of Cotton Mather to a logical conclusion. For if any sign not perfectly integrated with the Logos is evil, then there is something of evil in every sign. This treatment of the trope as an object is analogous to Mather's insistence on citing aphorisms even as the ones he cited advised against it, and to his insistence on the propriety of the word even when the words denied it. The work of French writers reflects no similar perspective in the nineteenth century. Hawthorne, and indeed all the great American writers of the century save Poe, had overcome the puritan fear of "magick spells," though they continued to identify literature with witchcraft as Mather had.

> I have experienced, that fancy is then [on a rainy day] most successful in imparting distinct shapes and vivid colors to the objects which the author has spread upon his page, and that his words become *magic spells* to summon up a thousand varied pictures. Strange landscapes glimmer through the familiar walls of the room, and outlandish figures thrust themselves almost within the sacred precincts of the hearth. (Hawthorne, *Tales,* 549)

The consequence of having condemned trope in favor of type results in a nineteenth-century fascination with the trope as a literary object. And the old view of the unintegrated sign as witchcraft endures, very visibly in the work of Hawthorne, less evidently elsewhere. *The Scarlet Letter* is nothing but a meditation on the trope of transgression—the hieroglyph of sin (pure trope), the letter *A*. The heraldic *motto* (Italian for "word") is an ancestor of the aphorism; a family's crest was supposed to be a kind of pictographic epigram which its motto translated, reflecting the clan's genetic and circumstantial history and aspirations. *The Scarlet Letter* ends by quoting a motto, translated into heraldic pictogram and retranslated into words.

> . . . one tombstone served for both. All around, there were monuments carved with armorial bearings; and on this simple slab of

slate—as the curious investigator may still discern, and perplex himself with the purport—there appeared the semblance of an engraved escutcheon. It bore a device, a herald's wording of which might serve for a motto and brief description of our now concluded legend; so sombre is it, and relieved only by one ever-glowing point of light gloomier than the shadow:—

"*On a field, sable, the letter A, gules.*" (*Novels*, 345)

Similarly, the great white whale of Herman Melville's imagination:

Is it that by its indefiniteness [the "vague, nameless horror" of the whale's whiteness] it shadows forth the heartless voids and immensities of the universe, and thus stabs us from behind with the thought of annihilation, when beholding the white depths of the milky way? Or is it, that as an essence whiteness is not so much a color as the visible absence of all colors; is it for these reasons that there is such a dumb blackness, full of meaning, in a wide landscape of snows—a colorless, all-color of atheism from which we shrink? (169)

Poe is more like his puritan precursors in enacting, even as he condemns, the witchcraft, the instability of rhetoric, than either Melville or Hawthorne. He continued to proclaim the very stoutest belief in the perfect integration of the word, for instance in *The Philosophy of Composition, The Rationale of Verse,* and *The Poetic Principle.* "It is my design," he wrote in *The Philosophy of Composition,* "to render it manifest that no point in its composition [that of "The Raven"] is referable either to accident or intuition—that the work proceeded step by step, to its completion with the precision and rigid consequences of a mathematical problem" (quoted in Symons, 178). He believed in the perfect unity of subject and literary object through perception, just as Edwards and Mather had, and he condemned rhetoric in the most unequivocal terms, as for example in this commentary on a poem of Elizabeth Barrett Browning.

Now here, saying nothing of the affectation in "adown"; not alluding to the insoluble paradox of "far yet near"; not mentioning the inconsistent metaphor involved in the sowing of fiery echoes; adverting but slightly as to the misuse of "like" in place of "as"; and to the impropriety of making anything fall like *thunder*, which has never been known to fall at all; merely hinting, too, at the misapplication of "steep" to the "generations" instead of to the "stairs" (a perver-

sion in no degree justified by the fact that so preposterous a figure
as synechdoche exists in the school-books . . . (quoted in Symons,
185–86)

The consequence was that Poe embodied, in his writings and in
his personality, the most extreme paradoxicality, the most violent
rhetoric, embracing science while condemning industry, extolling
logic as he flirted with mystery. Julian Symons has written that "part
of Poe wished to preserve poetry as a sacred mystery; another part
wanted to demonstrate that the whole thing was a technical problem,
which could be solved as one solves a cryptogram. These two parts
might be termed Visionary Poe and Logical Poe" (177). And Poe
too, like Arthur Gordon Pym, his fictional creation, is compelled
to confront, as the final source and subject of his literary quest, the
pure trope, the anti-antitype: "there arose in our pathway a shrouded
human figure, very far larger in its proportion than any dweller among
men. And the hue of the skin of the figure was of the perfect whiteness of snow" (Poe, *Works*, 242). Pym and his companion Peters
had discovered some subterranean markings whose significance is
precisely that they cannot be read or even ascertained with certainty
to reflect any human subjectivity.

> We were about leaving this fissure, into which very little light was
> admitted, when Peters called my attention to a range of singular looking
> indentures in the surface of the marl forming the termination of the
> cul-de-sac. With a very slight exertion of the imagination, the left,
> or most northern of these indentures might have been taken for the
> intentional, although rude, representation of a human figure standing
> erect, with outstretched arm. The rest of them bore also some little
> resemblance to alphabetical characters, and Peters was willing, at all
> events, to adopt the idle opinion that they were really such. (225)

A later gloss by the narrative's "editor," appended as a note to the
text, relates these figures to a word in Arabic meaning "to be white,"
compounding to exponentially dizzy extremity the pregnant emptiness of the sign in question; white, of course, as Melville pointed
out, is both absence and surfeit of color, chromatic significance.
Poe, like Mather, condemns witchcraft (obscurity, illogic) only to
be compelled to write about it, and in writing it, to enact it.

The split between Anglo-American and continental literary practice, so clear in the difference between the Puritans and Pascal,
continues to have repercussions in contemporary criticism. American critics like Hilton Kramer and Alfred Kazin condemn the French-

associated school of deconstruction, which really involves no more than a kind of close reading that accepts the importance and instability of rhetoric, in precisely the same way that Cotton Mather cried out, in the throes of puritan insecurity, against the spells of witches. The anachronistic resistance of such Americans (the English, it should be admitted, are even more wildly Francophobic) to a rhetorical dimension in criticism is really comparable only to the zealous hysteria of seventeenth-century witchhunters. Deconstruction sees the sign as groundless, Logosless, a causeless effect. It points once again to the necessity of mediation between subject and object, to the transparency of the sign, to the integrity of perception, as illusions grounded in narrow and fragile convention.

Louis Rubin, though far less known than Kramer or Kazin (for reasons evident in his crude misconstrual of structuralism below) typifies, albeit in parody, the new witch-hunters.

> . . . the fundamental premise of the New Criticism, whatever its wide variety of approaches to literature, is that the essential job of the critic is to prepare us to read the poem, whereas that of structuralism [a catch-all word by which Rubin denotes virtually any alien critical perspective] is that this not only shouldn't but can't be done, and that what the critic perforce does is to recreate the poem in his own image. It is an important difference, because your working New Critic willingly and by conviction subordinates his personality to the authority of the poem he is reading, preferring to let the text of the poem itself authenticate the terms of his response, while the structuralist views that as an unwarranted limitation on his own experience, and he grants no such authority—or authority as he might put it—to those verbal signs on the printed page. The choice is between humility and arrogance. Needless to say, I prefer the former. (21–22)

> As I understand it, the theory of structuralism would have it that the poem or the story, having no identity beyond that of a system of signs, can have no existence except insofar as the signs are decoded by the reader. What the reader does, therefore, is to give existence to the work by making it his own work: he breaks down the system of signs and reconstructs it in order to display its functions. To the verbal object that is the work, he adds intellect; the result is a simulacrum, in which the functions are made intelligible. (19–20)

Here we see the critic, bumblingly unaware, describing the bankruptcy of his own discourse as he loudly projects it onto an adversary who never existed as described. Structuralism and its more subtle, distant cousin, deconstruction, have never been anything but close reading, skilled and relentless explication (as Barbara Johnson put it, a "teasing out" of the text) which has the utmost respect—humility—before the ephemeral treacherousness, the power, of literature. What Rubin gives voice to is precisely an arrogance of ignorance, condemning something which he fears to understand. Anything which questions the unity, the transparency of the literary sign must be condemned, yet nothing does so more than the very act of interpretation, criticism itself. So Rubin is condemning his own enterprise, the very close reading, respect for the sign, which he purports to extol. Deconstruction is his Moby-Dick, his adulterous, scarlet-lettered alter ego, his devil-haunted manuscript, which he throws into the grate without any result but to have its implications sprout forth, multitudinous, in his own words. Melville and Hawthorne aped puritan rhetoric ironically, but critics like Rubin, even when more subtle and better informed, regress to puritanism. Just as Mather did in quoting La Bruyère, Rubin convicts himiself as he quotes from Robert Penn Warren's essay on "The Rime of the Ancient Mariner."

> . . . "a poem works immediately upon us when we are ready for it. And it may require the mediation of a great deal of critical activity by ourselves and by others before we are ready. And for the greater works we are never fully ready. That is why criticism is a never-ending process." In other words, the purpose of literary criticism is to enable us to experience the work of literature with greater richness and depth than might otherwise be possible. (19)

Of course what Warren points to in saying that the greatest literature is never transparent, can never be entirely integrated with our experience of it, is the most basic premise of deconstruction: the innate instability of literary language. Rubin, by calling himself a critic, by writing criticism, admits what he so obstreperously denies ("Methinks the lady doth protest too much"): that no text is perfectly clear, no perception can be unmediated, no reading can be definitive. "Get thee behind me devil, while I cast some spells."

Far more important than Rubin, who is to be understood here as a hyperbole, is the resurgence of a puritanical and moralistic mentality in the guise of Marxist literary criticism. In the criticisms lodged by Gerald Graff and Frank Lentricchia against Paul de Man, there is the same revealing opposition that we saw in Rubin between humility and arrogance. In *After the New Criticism,* for instance, Lentricchia entitles his chapter on de Man "The Rhetoric of Authority." Indeed it is an apt title, but more for Lentricchia himself than de Man. Graff and Lentricchia cannot tolerate what they see as a refusal by de Man to "argue in any formal sense for the logic and truth of his position" (Lentricchia, 293). They read him as exempting himself from the "undecidability" which he finds at the heart of literary language. If these readings of de Man were correct, he would indeed be guilty of arrogance. But they are wrong in a most revealing way, as was Rubin—wrong because they cannot allow themselves to take two things seriously: the importance of de Man's own rhetoric and the concept of the "undecidability of undecidability" in literature, which grounds all the assertions that they find groundless. As Barbara Johnson, de Man's student, put it:

> The "undeterminable" is not opposed to the determinable; "dissemination" is not opposed to repetition. If we could be sure of the difference between the determinable and the undeterminable, the undeterminable would be comprehended within the determinable. What is undecidable is whether a thing is decidable or not. (*CD,* 146)

The rhetoric of de Man's most important assertions is always very much like Pascal's, self-erasing, self-corrosive. The aphoristic chiasmus by which de Man characterized Proust's writing might apply just as well to his own: "*A la recherche du temps perdu* narrates the flight of meaning, but this does not prevent its own meaning from being, incessantly, in flight" (*A o R,* 78). The consequences of misreading de Man so gravely are myriad; one of the most absurd is the assertion that literature in de Man's view is closed off, self-contained. The hidden wish expressed here is, again, to repress the whole issue of an irony of irony, an undecidable undecidability, which is so threatening precisely because it cannot be contained, and thereby to reduce deconstruction to a fresh incarnation of the New Criticism of Ransom, Brooks, and Warren. This is precisely how Lentricchia and Graff wish to read deconstruction—wrongly but safely. If deconstruction could be said to have any authority, it would have to be a kind of apersonal, antiauthorial antiauthority stemming from the concept of an irony of irony. No conventionally Marxist critic will confront this as anything but witchcraft, "crafty rhetorical maneuvers" (Lentricchia, 293), because it puts the authority of Marxism—or of any other ism—into irremediable question. Just as we saw in Rubin's case, the two charges leveled against de Man are really reflexive confessions of guilt finding the only expression they can, through projection. The assertion of a "real" political and therefore moral content in literature; of a "political unconscious" (a grossly simple-minded contradiction in terms, by the way, as the unconscious cannot by definition be qualified as political, literary, or anything else); or of literature as subordinate to history and to a historical morality (a conclusion which promotes literary history over the actual reading of texts)—all these tenets of literary Marxism are what in fact cannot stand without an authoritarianism, a dogma like that of the Puritans, an arrogance which at its worst may approach intellectual fascism. But as always, insecurity is the reason for such stridency: the fear that what de Man performs, enacts in his essays, those "[witch]crafty rhetorical maneuvers," may reach out to engulf even the purest, the most stalwart and upstanding comrade.

3

Aphorism and Literary Epistemology:
Maurice Blanchot, Paul de Man, and Marcel Proust

Le pòete est celui qui entend un langage sans entente.
—BLANCHOT

We do not see what we love, but we love in the hope of confirming the illusion that we are indeed seeing anything at all.
—DE MAN

Les rêves ne sont pas réalisables, nous le savons; nous n'en formerions pas peut-être sans le désir, et il est utile d'en former pour les voir échouer et que leur échec instruise.
—PROUST

Maurice Blanchot, Marcel Proust, and Paul de Man share a tendency to aphoristic formulation. Maximlike sentences glow and bristle in the works of all three as highly charged nodes of rhetorical tension. Tracing the differences as well as the likenesses in the rhetoric of their common places (*sic*) as Blanchot reads Proust or de Man reads Blanchot and Proust (de Man inscribing himself as *the* textual tegument here) reveals something essential and often overlooked about Blanchot in particular and the commonplace in general.

That aphorism should be the point of juncture of these three should not surprise, given the nature of aphoristic discourse as an achieved disjunction of common knowledge and original observation. Aphorism enacts itself in a negative space of tension—between the universal and the particular, the anecdotal, the incidental, the common, and truth on the grandest scale. That truth never appears as a positive value in any good maxim or commonplace; rather, it subtends the verbal equation, inflecting each of its parts with a negative charge—negative, because opposed to their contingency, particularity. Thus the genre of the maxim *is* paradox, inasmuch as it tends to erode the logocentrism from which it first sprang, the credence in a bedrock of truth, underlying all thought and reality, which could be apprehended and stated within the bounds of language. In the opposition of universality and originality, totality (self-contained whole) and fragment, objective reality and subjective consciousness, the aphoristic discourse transpires ideally (and impossibly) as a play, an objectless desire, an aporia, an illusion, an oneiric absence, prestidigitation, oxymoron. (Each of these descriptions applies, thematically or rhetorically, to one or another of the statements cited above.) Thus it would offer Blanchot an ideal medium of communication, in which the totalized self is deconstructed in favor of the text, "not as if it were a thing, but as an autonomous entity, a 'consciousness without a subject'" (de Man, *B & I,* 78).

> Ceux qui s'en rendent compte et peu à peu reconnaissent qu'ils ne peuvent pas se connaître, mais seulement se transformer et se détruire, et qui poursuivent cet étrange combat où ils se sentent attirés hors d'eux-mêmes, dans un lieu où ils n'ont cependent pas accès, nous ont laissé, selon leurs forces, des *fragments,* d'ailleurs parfois impersonels, que l'on peut préférer à toute autre oeuvre. (*L à V,* 276–77)

> Those who realize it and little by little recognize that they cannot know themselves but only transform and destroy themselves, and who pursue that strange combat in which they feel drawn out of themselves into a place to which they do not, however, have access, have left us, according to their force, *fragments,* sometimes quite impersonal, which may be preferred to any other work.

Whatever is fragmentary in literature, and yet pretends to a certain positive or negative wholeness, has a necessary and logical connection with the aphoristic. We may as well note, in close proximity to the above statement by Blanchot, that de Man, his reader, never really wrote a book, but only collections of essays, fragments. This sort of text would offer de Man as well a medium in which to enact the negative force of irony, the pure discontinuity and self-contradictoriness of the literary word. Both Blanchot and de Man have

recognized something similar in Proust's treatment of human desire—thematically, perhaps, the best analogue of de Man-like irony
or Blanchot-like communication. In all three, aphoristic writing appears as the symptom of a common obsession with a certain anti-
thetical order of communication which each sees as the essence of
literariness and which cannot be described directly but only framed
by repetition. That repetition most often takes the form of aphoristic
language.

> Mallarmé's faith in the progressive development of self-conscious-
> ness, for example, must be abandoned, since every new step in this
> progression turns out to be a regression toward a more and more
> remote past. Yet it remains possible to speak of a certain develop-
> ment, of a movement of becoming that persists in the fictional world
> of literary invention. In a purely temporal world, there can be no
> perfect repetition, as when two points coincide in space . . . And
> elsewhere [Blanchot writes]: "We necessarily always write the same
> thing over again, but the development of what remains the same has
> infinite richness in its very repetition." (de Man, *B & I*, 75–76)

In elaborating the privileged moments of (virtual) temporal repetition in Proust, Blanchot points, without seeming to realize it entirely, to a parallel between involuntary memory and the common
place, the *lieu (en) commun*. In both there occurs a threat of abolition of subjectivity, of originality (inasmuch as the concept of originality is grounded in the concept of subjectivity). The aphoristic
text depends, for its effectiveness, on being apprehended as perfectly true, perfectly applicable, perfectly relevant in and to the present
moment, to the individual who is reading the text in the present
moment. Yet it must at the same time suscitate the sense of having
been so to many other readers, and to at least one writer, at other
moments of the past. Thus ideally, the moment of reading an aphorism is a moment of Blanchot-like *ressassement,* of infinite repetition, a moment in which past and present become, or threaten to
become, perfectly specular, and remembrance is virtually identical
with oblivion, because what is remembered is not something which
happened but something which is happening (the act of reading),
which, however, can have significance only as something that has
always been happening. De Man says very correctly, then, that
"Blanchot's criticism, starting out as an ontological meditation, leads
back into the question of the temporal self" (*B & I*, 76).

Blanchot himself established the link between Proustian involuntary memory, the moment in which the *être de mort*, as Proust called it, finds its sustenance, and the *lieu commun*. For the place in which the universal and the particular, the past and the present, objectivity and subjectivity, join hands, is the *common place* as the place of otherness, the other place.

> L'expérience du temps imaginaire qu'a faite Proust ne peut avoir lieu que dans un temps imaginaire et en faisant de celui qui s'y expose un être imaginaire, une image errante, toujours là, toujours absente, fixe et convulsive, comme la beauté dont André Breton a parlé. Métamorphose du temps, elle métamorphose d'abord le présent où elle semble se produire, l'attirant dans la profondeur indéfinie où le "présent" recommence le "passé", mais où le passé s'ouvre à l'avenir qu'il répète, pour ce qui vient, toujours revienne, et à nouveau, à nouveau. Certes, la révélation a lieu maintenant, ici, pour la première fois, mais l'image qui nous est présente ici et pour la première fois, est présence d'un "déjà une autre fois", et ce qu'elle nous révèle, c'est que "maintenant" est "jadis", et ici, encore un autre lieu, un lieu toujours autre où celui qui croit pouvoir assister tranquillement du dehors à cette transformation, ne peut la transformer en pouvoir que s'il se laisse tirer par elle hors de soi et entraîner dans ce mouvement où une partie de lui-même, et d'abord cette main qui écrit, devient comme imaginaire. (Blanchot, *L à V*, 29)

> Proust's experience of imaginary time can occur only in an imaginary time and by making whoever exposes himself to it into an imaginary being, a fleeting image, always there, always absent, fixed, and convulsive, like the beauty that André Breton talked about. A metamorphosis of time, it metamorphoses first the present in which it appears to be produced, drawing it into the indefinite depth in which the "present" recommences the "past," but where the past opens up to a future which it repeats, for that which comes must always come back, and again and again. Certainly, the revelation is taking place now, here, for the first time, but the image which is present to us here and for the first time is the presence of an "already once before," and what it reveals to us is that "now" is "before," and here yet another place, always another place where anyone who believes he can calmly stand by as a witness outside this transformation can only translate the revelation into power if he allows it to draw him out of himself and into this movement in which a part of himself, and first of all this hand that writes, becomes as though imaginary.

The idea of commonplaces as ports of call on the student's or the orator's itinerary (first formulated in Aristotle's *Topica*) is reflected further in Blanchot's use of the Ulysses myth in *Le Livre à venir*, his insistence on navigation as a metaphor for writing, for the *chant des sirènes:*

> Il y avait quelque chose de merveilleux dans ce chant réel, chant *commun,* secret, chant simple et quotidien, qu'il leur fallait tout à coup reconnaître, chanté irréellement par des puissances étrangères et, pour le dire, imaginaires, chant de l'abîme qui, une fois entendu, ouvrait dans chaque parole un abîme et invitait fortement à y disparaître. (*L à V,* 10; my emphasis)

> There was something fantastic in this real song, this *common* and secret song, this simple, ordinary song, that they had no choice but to suddenly recognize, sung unreally by strange and even imaginary powers, a song from the abyss which, once heard, would open up an abyss in each and every word and invite one most powerfully to disappear into it.

Of Blanchot's own aphoristic rhetoric I will have more to say later.

Proust, on the other hand, does not appear to lend credence to the possibility of self-deconstruction, short of death. Indeed, in describing the experience of involuntary memory, he sets up a dialectic between death and chance (the chance by which involuntary memory is triggered), between certainty and relativity, which is perfectly analogous to the tension of the universal and the particular, the global and the fragmentary, that one finds in the theory and practice of the aphorism. "Il y a beaucoup de hasard en tout ceci, et un second hasard, celui de notre mort, souvent ne nous permet pas d'attendre longtemps les faveurs du premier" (I, 44). "There is a great deal of chance in all this, and a second chance, that of our death, often does not allow us to wait long for the favors of the first.") Death, a sort of totalization or integral of chance, must be none other than truth, Logos, and it puts an end to all apprehension of itself. It cannot be known directly, unmitigatedly. In this way Proust is either a bit more subtle or less paradoxical than his reader Blanchot: The Abolition of the Subject (Blanchot's Truth or transcendental Signified) can have meaning, can be represented within language and within living consciousness, only through the mediation of fragmentary, haphazard signifiers which dilute it, render its poison less than fatally intoxicating. The pure literary experience, like that of involuntary memory (which is a metaphor, or perhaps a metonymy, for the former), is a threat of death, of the abolition of temporal difference, which depends for the pleasure it affords on not being consummated—rather like the dialectic of Eros and Thanatos, in which the pleasure principle seeks a reduction of tension (Eros) in the organism, but only short of zero, the point at which Eros disappears and only the stasis of Thanatos remains. Perhaps Proust merely states the same paradox differently from Blanchot: Rather than as a consciousness without a subject (a sort of epistemological catachresis), Proust sees literary experience as a kind of apprehension of the atemporality of death within the temporality of life, holding back, unlike Blanchot, from even a polemical embrace of atemporality as possible or desirable.

Blanchot recognizes this dialectic in Proust, describing it as a tension of two sorts of temporality.

> Temps d'abord réel, destructeur, le Moloch effrayant qui produit la mort et la mort de l'oubli . . . Le temps est capable d'un tour plus étrange. Tel incident insignifiant, qui a eu lieu à un certain moment, jadis donc, oublié, et non seulement oublié, inaperçu, voici que le cours du temps le ramène, et non pas comme un souvenir, mais comme un fait réel, qui a lieu à nouveau, à un nouveau moment du temps. Ainsi le pas qui trébuche sur les pavés mal équarris de la cour de Guermantes est tout à coup—rien n'est plus soudain—le pas même qui a trébuché sur les dalles inégales du Baptistère de Saint-Marc: le même pas, non pas "un double, un écho d'une sensation passée . . . mais cette sensation elle-même," incident infime, bouleversant, qui déchire la trame du temps et par cette déchirure nous introduit dans un autre monde: hors du temps, dit Proust avec précipitation. (L à V, 22)

> First real, destructive time, the terrifying Moloch which produces death and the death of oblivion. . . . This time is capable of something even stranger. Such and such an insignificant event, which occurred at a certain moment, past then, forgotten, and not only forgotten but unnoticed, here the course of time brings it back, and not as a recollection but as a real fact which happens anew in a new moment of time. Thus the step which stumbles on the ill-cut stones of the Guermantes courtyard is suddenly—nothing is more sudden— the same step which stumbled on the irregular flagstones of the Baptistery of Saint Mark's: the same step, not "a double, an echo of a

past sensation . . . but the sensation itself," a minute, convulsive incident which rips the woof of time and by that tear introduces us into another world: outside time, says Proust precipitously.

Blanchot, however, goes considerably further than Proust in elaborating this moment. For Proust it is virtual, ebbing even as it reaches greatest intensity, as the analytic faculties of intelligence reach out to enclose, preserve, describe it. Proust's "homme affranchi de l'ordre du temps" never comes into full being; he is an "être de mort." For Blanchot, even if it is paradoxical, grounded in a (dis)juncture of two different kinds of time, this moment is pure, ecstatic: "Voici donc le temps effacé par le temps lui-même; voici la mort, cette mort qui est l'oeuvre du temps, suspendue, neutralisée, rendue vaine et inoffensive" (*L à V,* 22–23). ("Here then is time erased by time itself; here is death, that death which is the work of time, suspended, neutralized, rendered vain and inoffensive.") Blanchot rushes headlong into an exclamatory rhetoric of optimism verging on sentimentality, affirming that this dialectic of time and untime can realize itself within the *oeuvre* as a negation of the negation of death. He can do so only by describing death not as atemporality but rather as the essence of the order of time, something for which there is ample precedent in Proust, though again it does not coincide entirely with the latter's view of death as an "integral" of time and therefore its antithesis. Death is not, for Blanchot, pure negativity. That distinction is reserved in his reading for the suspension and the tension of involuntary memory. Yet by turning this tension into a kind of absolute, the Other of temporality, Blanchot obliterates its difference from death and its power as a momentary escape from death's chronological imperative (an escape that is incomplete, unconsummated, for to consummate it is indeed to turn it into death).

Death, in Blanchot's view, is a linguistic apprehension of death rather than a pure negativity which would defy representation or even thought. Blanchot is able to embrace that pure negativity (real death) in a burst of exclamations because he has located it within the signifying realm of temporal consciousness.

> Vivre l'abolition du temps, vivre ce mouvement, rapide comme l'"éclair", par lequel deux instants, infiniment séparés, viennent (*peu à peu quoique aussitôt*) à la rencontre l'un de l'autre, s'unissant comme deux présences qui, par la métamorphose du désir, s'identifieraient,

c'est parcourir toute la réalité du temps, en la parcourant éprouver
le temps comme espace et lieu vide, c'est-à-dire libre des évènements
qui toujours ordinairement le remplissent. Temps pur, sans évènements,
vacance mouvante, distance agitée, espace intérieur en devenir où
les extases du temps se disposent en une simultanéité fascinante,
qu'est-ce donc que tout cela? Mais le temps même du récit, le temps
qui n'est pas *hors* du temps, mais qui s'éprouve comme *dehors*, sous
la forme d'un espace, cet espace imaginaire où l'art trouve et dispose
ses ressources. (*L à V*, 23)

To live the abolition of time, to live this moment, rapid as "light-
ning," by which two instants, infinitely separated, come (little by
little, though all at once) to meet each other, uniting like two pres-
ences which, by the metamorphosis of desire, would identify each
other and themselves, this is to traverse all the reality of time, and
in traversing it to feel time as space and empty place, that is to say
free from events which always ordinarily fill it. Pure time without
event, moving vacancy, agitated distance, interior space in process
of becoming, in which the ecstasies of time dispose themselves in a
fascinating simultaneity, what is all that, after all? What but the time
of story, time which is not *outside* time but experienced as *outside*
it in the form of a space, that imaginary space where art finds and
disposes its resources.

Proust is far more cautious, and closer in spirit to the great aphorists (La Rochefoucauld, Chamfort), because the Logos, the coincidence of universal and particular, death (the "outside" of time),
and time are always virtual, always fail, and should fail, for the
sake of the pleasure that they afford and that one seeks in them—
the pleasure of the literary text, or of desire. De Man expresses this
succinctly:

Marcel is never as far away from Proust as when the latter has him
say: "Happy are those who have encountered truth before death and
for whom, however close it may be, the hour of truth has rung before
the hour of death." As a writer, Proust is the one who knows that
the hour of truth, like the hour of death, never arrives on time, since
what we call time is precisely truth's inability to coincide with itself.
A la recherche du temps perdu narrates the flight of meaning, but
this does not prevent its own meaning from being, incessantly, in
flight. (*A o R*, 78)

One might begin to scrutinize de Man's own aphoristic rhetoric
by noting, in the above, the highly epigrammatic formulation, the

nearly perfect form of chiasmus: "flight of meaning . . . meaning
. . . in flight." This reversal sets up virtuality, a tension much like
Proust's, which holds back from Blanchot's ideal of death within
the text while hovering within astoundingly close range of it, in the
very arc of current separating time and untime, representation and
truth, consciousness and death. That reversal does not account for
three terms in the sentence which, left behind as a residue of the
chemistry of reversal, are juxtaposed as somehow equivalent, parallel, within the equation: the verbs "to narrate," "to prevent," and
"to be." Narration, existence, and prevention—a cautiousness, a
holding back (from an optimism, rhetorical or real, which would
leap, or feign to leap, into the open arms of the abyss)—thus remain
as the poles among which volts of meaning and flight sputter and
crackle.

Yet the difference between Blanchot and Proust, and between
Blanchot and de Man, is really one of style, rhetoric, and degree.
Blanchot exhibits an exuberance in paradox, a brazen glee in the
face of the negativity at the heart of the literary work, yet he never
fulfills this happy (even smug) threat to disappear into the heart of
darkness, though he often reminds us of the possibility, rather like
a juggler of butcher knives informing his audience in gory detail of
the risk involved in his entertainment of them.

> Ecrire sans "écriture", amener la littérature à ce point d'absence où
> elle disparaît, où nous n'avons plus à redouter ses secrets qui sont
> des mensonges, c'est là "le degré zéro de l'écriture", la neutralité
> que tout écrivain recherche délibérément ou à son insu et qui conduit
> quelques-uns au silence. (*L à V*, 303)

> To write without "writing," to bring literature to that point of ab-
> sence where it disappears, where we no longer need dread its secrets
> which are lies, this is the "zero degree of writing," the neutrality
> which every writer seeks, deliberately or unknowingly, and which
> leads some to silence.

So, as his paradoxes are less subtle, more extreme, Blanchot dips
even closer to nothingness than Proust or de Man, but perhaps he
does not hover at the point of least distance and greatest tension so
long as either of them. Thus he is able to sustain an affirmativeness
beyond both Proust and de Man.

> Nous devons d'abord essayer de rassembler quelques-uns des traits

que l'approche de l'espace littéraire nous a permis de reconnaître. Là, le langage n'est pas un pouvoir, il n'est pas le pouvoir de dire. Il n'est pas disponible, en lui nous ne disposons de rien. Il n'est jamais le langage que je parle. En lui, je ne parle jamais, jamais je ne m'adresse à toi, et jamais je ne t'interpelle. Tous ces traits sont de forme négative. Mais cette négation masque seulement le fait plus essentiel que dans ce langage *tout retourne à l'affirmation,* que ce qui nie, en lui affirme. C'est qu'il parle comme absence. Là où il ne parle pas, déjà il parle; quand il cesse, il persévère. Il n'est pas silencieux, car précisément le silence en lui se parle. Le propre de la parole habituelle, c'est que l'entendre fait partie de sa nature. Mais, en ce point de l'espace littéraire, le langage est sans entente. De là le risque de la fonction poétique. Le poète est celui qui entend un langage sans entente. (*L'E l,* 51)

We ought first to try to reassemble some of the traits which the approach to literary space has allowed us to recognize. There, language is not a power, it is not the power of speech. It is not available, in it we control nothing. It is never the language which I speak. In it I never speak, never address myself to you, and never call upon you. All these traits are negative in form. But this negation masks only the more essential fact that in language *everything comes back to affirmation,* that that which denies, affirms in it. This is because it speaks as absence. There where it does not speak, it speaks already; when it ceases, it persists. It is not silent, because it is precisely silence which in it speaks itself. The property of the usual word is that comprehension is part of its nature. But in this point of literary space, language is without comprehension. Whence the risk of the poetic function. The poet is he who understands a language without understanding.

This affirmation is couched in the most epigrammatic language. And it is only through the lens of aphorism, the dialectic on which it turns, that the paradoxical optimism of Blanchot, his difference from his reader de Man and from Proust, whose text he read, is visible.

To return to the short texts with which this chapter began, the tension of aphoristic paradox in Proust is most often associated with the representation of desire, or of particular instances of desire such as dream, and it seems to act as a formal and specular metaphor of desire even as it *enacts* it rhetorically. De Man held the term *scholar* and those who revere it in utmost contempt, insisting on the incompatibility of literary theory and literary scholarship ["R t T," 4], yet for de Man the same is true as for Proust, with the qualification that de Man's emphasis, as someone assumed to be a scholar, is rather on understanding, or consciousness; but these are for him nothing but desire ("We do not see what we love"). The most frequent aphoristic style of Proust is parataxis, the juxtaposition of clauses within a sentence, building by apposition toward an epigrammatic paradox ("Les rêves ne sont pas réalisables"). De Man's characteristic figure is antimetabole or chiasmus, reversal, but always with a crucial extra term or terms left over—"illusion" and "hope," in this case: "we love in the hope of confirming the illusion." These extra terms name the tension which his language enacts. In de Man's vocabulary, any hope of confirmation is part of the illusion to which it is directed. Blanchot works in the stark, simple pattern of oxymoron, even non sequitur: "Le poète est celui qui entend un langage sans entente." Always the negation of a negation, which in Blanchot's work results in affirmation which is not the same as illusion. "cette négation masque seulement le fait plus essentiel que dans ce langage tout retourne à l'affirmation." ("This negation masks only the more essential fact that in this language anything comes back to affirmation.") This is possible for Blanchot because, for him, that negation remains within the space of representation, of consciousness; indeed, in both his vocabulary and his aphoristic gestures, it remains on the most stately, classically pure level of concepts. He does not stoop to the more unwieldy, messier terrain of desire, at least not as Proust and de Man do. This is not to say that he does not address the issue of desire, for of course he does. But it is always regarded as an idea, an abstraction, always as one large signifier, mesmerizingly lovely in its clean, simple lines even if it does threaten, like Mallarmé's absent flower or a great white shark, not a writhing, unclean chain of ill-matched signifiers, burgeoning grotesquely at both ends and metamorphosing, chimeralike at every point—every particular, ordinary, nondescript, fragmentary point—in between.

But then, in a context of delirium, the only valid criteria of judging vantage points is surely to seek the one that affords the greatest pleasure. So Blanchot's affirmation might be the most authentically literary response to the monster of temporal being, death-in-life: to embrace it. To embrace an illusion, a failed dream—nothing—can surely do no harm.

4

Aphorism and Criticism:
Deconstruction and the Commonplace Tradition

We have already seen that aphoristic writing is a conceptually treacherous terrain. In the previous sentence, by assuming a metaphorical equivalency between place, a plot of land, a specific topography, and a kind of writing, I have enacted the venerable aporia on which the genre is based and which, indeed, all our ideas of truth and of the representation of truth must claim as ancestor. This same trope is repeated in the concept of the commonplace (a place which everyone knows) and, evidently, in the more distantly related word, *plot*. The word *commonplace,* as already mentioned, refers to a much revered tenet of classical rhetoric. Aristotle bears witness to the concept in his *Topica:* Acquiring knowledge or disseminating it is like being a tourist, a matter of going to the various places which are the knowledge in question. There are common places and specific ones, the latter only rarefied derivations of the former. This distinction—and by now it should be apparent that aphoristic writing seems always to suscitate such attempts at categorization, neat distinction, even as it confounds them in paradox—this distinction is repeated by such contemporaries of ours as Louis Kronenburger and W. H. Auden, editors of *The Viking Book of Aphorisms,* when they insist on a difference between epigram and aphorism: "An epigram need only be true of a single case . . . or effective only in a particular context . . . An aphorism, on the other hand, must convince every reader that it is either universally true or true of every member of the class to which it refers, irrespective of the reader's convictions" (v). This differential taxonomy is a matter of degree only, and serves to point out the extreme relativity implicit in the concept of universality. Nothing is universally universal. There is nothing which, scrutinized closely, will not betray some taint of particularity.

The common places are so called because they are (ideally) common to everyone and to all forms of knowledge. But all the places, inasmuch as they are rhetorical gestures, are forms as well as objects. Any place has both volume and at least the potential of a certain mass. *Place* refers as well by extension, in classical usage, to the various parts of an argument or exposition, which are nothing but the orderly transfer of knowledge to another. The places, and especially the common places, are both means and object of knowledge. They are the means of teaching and what it taught, memory and what is remembered. Here is Cicero:

> Persons desiring to train this faculty [the memory] must select *localities* and form mental images of the facts they wish to remember and store those images in the localities, with the result that the arrangement of the localities will preserve the order of the facts, and *the images of the facts will designate the facts themselves,* and we shall employ the localities and images respectively as a wax writing tablet and the letters written on it. (I, 467; my emphasis)

The teacher is rather like a tour guide. If he is any good, he takes us to the right places and tries to show them to us from the best vantage point. Why? So we can say we have been there, or take others there, or buy souvenirs and postcards to send friends—in a way, to prove that we were there—or take pictures which represent, which call back our memory of having been there. Cicero speaks of this as "that system of associating commonplaces with symbols," a procedure by which memory is "trained by carefully learning by heart as many pieces as possible both from our Latin writers and the foreigner." Can it surprise us that listening to a great orator should be described by Cicero through the metaphor of a house tour? Effective pedagogy is likewise described in terms of a well-conducted tour [I, 111]. So that the purpose of a voyage or tour is to acquire a sign, a trace of the locale, whether object or memory. The two-dimensional form of the pictorial image represents, substitutes for, erases the mass of the original. Its emptiness as form is complicated by its own (semiotically) superfluous mass and physical characteristics—the smell, heft, size, feel of the paper on which the image is printed. What good do they do us, these poor copies, traces of the original place? Remember that the places are not just object but means, not just mass but form. We may reach other places by way of them, by actually going through them to the other places beyond or by inferring the latter, inferring other, similar places from the ones we know. Or we may use our knowledge of the place to find our way back to it, or to bring others back to it—again, literally or in imagination, by showing them pictures.

What this by now rather overextended metaphor shows is how, in fact, the object is not an object, but constantly defers to other objects, or is an object of the tourist's approach to knowing only insofar as some other object (postcards, photos, souvenirs, themselves objects only in the same sense) may be substituted for it, or only insofar as it leads to other objects, other places. Place is only passage. No one brings the Tower of Pisa home with him, and most people would not want it in their living rooms, though the removal of bricks and bits of wood from famous sites betrays a rather primitive, fetishistic absence of sophistication at work in some minds: the failure to differentiate form and mass. The same fallacy, however, would be sublimated in the expensive Japanese or German camera dangling from the neck of the most sophisticated and well-heeled tourist. It is inescapable to a certain degree. We cannot conceive form without mass. But the simplistic thinking, or lack of it, behind the vandalism of monuments is an apt analogy for the attitude of some scholars of literature who, despite the implications of poststructuralist strategies of reading, continue to insist that the literary monument—Proust or Shakespeare or Whitman—not only can but ought to be transported into the classroom and the living room and, whole, entire, into the skulls of students. This constitutes a rather hallucinatory misconception, not just because the monuments themselves are in most cases deceased, no longer extant. Even if they were living, the authors themselves are not literature. It is their manuscripts, definitive editions, which would be the fetishes of those professional critics who style themselves "conservative," who see themselves as acting in the defense of tradition.

Yet even if we consider the definitive edition as the real place in question, it is not the objective materiality of the thing that counts—

the fact that it comprises so much ink and paper, or that someone put the ink on the paper in the first place and may have worn a hat and odd clothes when he did it, or had just engaged in some sexual act, perverted or otherwise: rather, what counts is what a reader makes of it. Precisely as in the case of the tourist, it is the going and seeing that makes the experience, not the object itself. Or, more subtly, it is the shape of the object as it is cast upon the eye's retina or the camera's film, its formal impingement upon a matter with which it has nothing to do beyond this momentary contingency, that matters, that is the truth of literary knowledge. This does not come down to a reader-response theory of literature. The subject is just as problematic in comprising matter and form, just as contingent, as what is reflected upon it, its object. This is more than evident in the repeated efforts of classical writers to assert a distinction between form and content, learning and character, which their teaching invariably contradicts. "In what," Cicero junior asks Cicero senior, "do the speaker's personal resources consist," as distinct from the other two aspects of oratory, the speech and the question? The first sentence of the elder Cicero's reply illustrates perfectly both the contradiction in question and the pretense of having resolved it, of having effectively sustained the distinction:

> [The speaker's personal resources consist] in matter and in language. But both matter and language have to be found and have to be arranged—although the term "invention" is used specifically of the matter and "delivery" of the language, but arrangement, though belonging to both, nevertheless is applied to invention. With delivery go voice, gesture, facial expression and general bearing, and all of these are in the keeping of memory. (II, 313)

These personal resources appear not too personal at all when interrogated closely. What this means is that there can be no clear, pure distinction between speaker and spoken, personal intention and impersonal rhetoric or, by the same logic, between reader and text, perceiver and perceived. When the tourist takes a photograph, he is attempting to capture his own vision, metonymically to capture himself. The need to supplement the object (the monument) with souvenirs of various kinds is a function of the object's and the subject's contingency, their failure to be self-sufficient. The entire experience, the terrain of subject or object, can never be adequately known, mapped. It can only be endlessly repeated, substituted for, erased, and recalled to mind by representation.

For writing, not only but perhaps more saliently in the aphoristic mode, the implications are far-reaching, and render moot a large part of the critical debate which has raged in literary studies over the past few years. So-called deconstruction, inasmuch as it assumes, in the most basic, epistemological fashion, the mutual involvement of object, subject, and representation, is less than any other school of critical thought guilty of what it is most often accused of—the divorce of literature from reality. In fact, when considered alongside the commonplace or aphoristic mode of literary discourse, deconstruction appears to be the true heir to tradition, far more conservative (in the truest sense of the word) than its antagonists. Literature—representation, repetition—contaminates reality (and vice versa) by its very nature. It needs no critical apparatus, whether moral or Marxist or subjective, to do so. Of course, by its nature it also compels such superfluous repetitions, and we shall not be surprised to find the tourists contending as to whose photographs are best. Each one takes a different kind of picture, but no camera, however cleverly made or specialized, makes possible the phenomenon of specularity. Rather the other way around.

Aphoristic writing makes this more than evident because, in my estimation, it is, in a number of ways, a hyperbolic exemplar of writing in general. If we interrogate the various other synonyms for commonplace, we can see that all repeat the concept of the common place, remaining consistent with the metaphor of place, the metonymy of the souvenir. Aphorism, for instance, first means nothing but "a distinction or a definition" (OED). Proverb, from *proverbum*, is simply a set of words put forth. Motto is nothing but italian for *word*. Epigram means, in Greek, to write upon, an *inscription*. Here, in *to write upon*, we see *inscribed* the very arbitrariness and contingency of form and matter, sign and substance, image and beholder, object and subject, which I alluded to above. All these terms begin by assuming a truth or mass in the object which they pretend to extract and disseminate in po(r)table form. All begin as an inscription or commentary subordinated to, but ideally repetitious of, their object. Thus in the Middle Ages there was "the tendency to give each particular case the character of a moral sentence or of an example, so that it becomes something substantial and unchallengeable, the crystallization of thought . . ." And "in the same way every utterance becomes a dictum, a maxim, a text" (Huizinga, 229, 227). This came directly from classical tradition. Isocrates, for instance, wrote that

> he [the orator] will select from all the actions of men which bear upon his subject those examples which are the most illustrious and the most edifying; and, habituating himself to contemplate and appraise such examples, he will feel their influence not only in the preparation of a given discourse but in all the actions of his life. (cited in Lechner, 6)

The assumption of a weightiness, a great density of mass in these brief, formal repetitions (expressed in the origin of the word *maxim*— from *maxima sententia,* the greatest wisdom in the smallest space, a paradoxical coincidence of particularity and supposed universality), is belied by their role as common*places,* rhetorical embellishments. This too is a concept with a classical pedigree. You cannot hope to lead someone to a new, unknown point except by conducting him there through an itinerary which is in some way or other pleasingly familiar. Here is Quintillian:

> In arguments of a minor character the language and thought should be as appropriate and as familiar as possible. But if the subject be one of real importance every kind of ornament should be employed, . . . the more unattractive the natural appearance of anything, the more does it require to be seasoned by charm of style; moreover, an argument is often less suspect when thus disguised, and the charm with which it is expressed makes it all the more convincing to our audience. (Lechner, 4–5)

And yet upon this point the mass and form of the object, familiar substance and rhetorical flourish, begin to become divorced. In Quintillian we see eloquence defined in terms of commonplace, and the supposed substance of truth dissolving into the empty form of figure.

> I do not use this term in its usual acceptance, namely, commonplaces directed against luxury, adultery, and the like, but in the sense of the secret places where arguments reside, and from which they must be drawn forth. (Lechner, 25–26)

The same tendency is visible in Apthonius, here translated by Rainold.

> A Common place is a Oracion, dilatyng and amplifyng good or evill, whiche is incidente or lodged in any man. This Oracion is called a common place, because the matter conteined in it, doeth agree uniuersally to all menne, whiche are partakers of it, and giltie of the same. (Lechner, 17)

A commonplace can by its nature apply to many different objects, not just the one on which it was originally based. This makes its mass suspect, to say the least. Its truth depends on how it is used, to what object it is applied. Thus it renders problematic the very integrity of the object it repeats, not only by claiming to repeat it, but by involving it, contaminating it with all the other objects to which the commonplace may apply.

But the common place erodes not only the integrity of the object. The enunciating subject is equally affected, as of course it must be, if we are to admit the mutual contamination of the two categories, subjective and objective. Certainly classical theoreticians knew that the "places" were as necessary to the establishment of the subject as to his or her object. Quintillian, for instance, writes that "the instruments which I have mentioned are the instruments not of the art but of the orator himself" (I, 318). Anyone may make a commonplace his own simply by repeating it—indeed, according to the classical idea, education is in large measure nothing but the transfer of the commonplaces into the minds of the young. Thus the commonplace is the very possibility, the grounding, of the concept of originality. Without a knowledge of the commonplaces, no one can be expected to express himself in a fashion which might merit being called winning or elegant or original. "What need," writes Cicero, "to speak of that universal treasure-house, the memory? Unless this faculty be placed in charge of the ideas and phrases which have been thought out and well-weighed, even though as conceived by the orator they were of the highest excellence, we know that they will all be wasted." (I, 15).

So that, just as knowledge of the commonplaces may be used to project or imagine other places, to make new arguments and invent new discourses, so the same knowledge, the same knowing, is used to project and achieve the illusion of distinct authorial subjectivities. If a speaking or writing subject does not demonstrate a knowledge of the common places, he will be taken as ignorant, beneath the category of originality, and if he uses them improperly, like a tourist who confuses his picture postcard of the Eiffel Tower with the thing itself (or his wife or the toilet), he will be thought mad. Proper knowledge of the common place demands a common attitude toward it. Those who transgress, if short of insanity but beyond ignorance, will be stigmatized as vandals or neurotics, plagiarists or cliché-mongers. Quintillian writes that "the chief signs of [oratorical] ability are a good memory and the power of imitation, though the latter should not degenerate into malicious mimicry" (I, 32). Neil Hertz has written that

> Just as the masturbation of children can serve to focus the anxiety of their elders about sexuality in general, so the plagiarizing of students can focus their teachers' anxieties about writing in general, more particularly about the kind of "writing" involved in teaching—the inscription of a culture's heritage on the minds of its young. A teacher's uncertainty about (to cite the pamphlet [on student plagiarism] again) "whose words he is reading or listening to" begins, in the classroom, with his own words—and this would be true not merely for those colleagues we think of complacently as less original than ourselves. The recurrent touting of originality—in letters of recommendation, reports of *ad hoc* committees, etc.—is no doubt a sign of the same uneasiness that produces the ritual condemnation of student plagiarists when they are unlucky enough to be caught. (63)

What makes possible the projection of the subject, and of the object, must pose a potential menace to the stable aseity of both. If it is recognized as such, allowed to stray for even a moment from its prescribed, necessary, assumed, imposed, and forgotten place, that is, to appear from a vantage point unlike the acceptedly "common" one, the commonplace suddenly becomes plagiary or cliché or nonsense, taboo to a greater or lesser degree, depending on the extent to which it has been allowed to stray from its proper location. Of course nonsense is all right, so long as it admits that it is such. "Such jests," writes Aristotle, "in fact, play the part of maxims and admonitions" (409). Lewis Carroll's writings, for instance, are full of contorted commonplaces, deliberately misapplied. Such misapplications, by depending on and alluding to the proper common place, assert the stability of the latter even as they affect to play dangerously upon it. The trick may appear fraught with peril, but in fact it is performed over a net. Otherwise the commonplace might begin to threaten the concept of propriety. The word *proper* comes from the French *propre* and connotes possession. Thus "propriety" is inscribed in the notion of originality and is subject to the same epistemological difficulty. Recognized as the mirror by which the trick of originality, subjectivity, self, is achieved, propriety threatens not only the trick, its effect, but its own conceptual self. Tautologically, it is in the idea of the common place that the idea of the commonplace is grounded. Once questioned, there is no longer any propriety, no longer any place at all, distinct from any other place, except the place of the questioning, a place subject to perpetual dis-placement.

It seems appropriate at this juncture to scrutinize a highly relevant detail in Molière's *School for Wives*. It can be no accident that the would-be pedagogue of this play tries to use a book of maxims to prevent his pupil Agnès' apprehension not only of certain positive knowledge but also of the manner in which he is preventing her apprehension of it. Under the guise of expanding her knowledge, the pupil would thus be induced to limit it. But the efficacy of this stratagem depends entirely on its success in concealing itself, in passing itself off as something which it is not. Here is Barbara Johnson's reading of the passage.

> The book Arnolphe assigns to Agnès is a book of Maxims on the Duties of the Married Woman. In typical teacherly fashion, he asks the student to read the book through carefully and promises to explain it to her when she has finished. The book contains a list not of duties but of interdictions: a wife belongs to no one but her husband; she should dress up only for him, receive no visitors but his, accept presents from no man, and never seek to do any writing, to join any feminine social circles, to visit the gambling table, or to go out on walks or picnics. In short, the book for the first time replaces the absence of teaching with the active teaching of the content of ignorance. In place of her former lack of knowledge, the pupil now possesses a knowledge of what she is not supposed to know . . .
>
> The similarity between the teachers *of* the text and the teacher *in* the text should give us pause. Could it be that the pedagogical enterprise as such is always constitutively a project of teaching ignorance? Are our ways of teaching students to ask *some* questions always correlative with our ways of teaching them *not to ask*—indeed, to be unconscious of—others? Does the educational system exist to promulgate knowledge, or is its main function rather to universalize

a society's tacit agreement about what it has decided it does not and cannot know? . . .

What Arnolphe wishes to exclude from Agnes's knowledge is play— here, the play of language for its own sake, the possibility that language could function otherwise than in strict obedience to the authority of proper meaning. (*"TI,"* 170–71, 173, 176)

Thus the commonplace or maxim or aphorism does not simply convey knowledge, teach in a positive sense. It teaches both positively and negatively. It tells us what we should know, but this positive knowledge excludes other possibilities of knowing. The commonplace must appear with all the innocence of self-evident truth in order to achieve both ends—it must offer a positive image of a place (object of knowledge) and it must supplant all possibility of a different image, thus forestalling any interrogation of the way in which it is related to, determined by, and determinative of this object which it pretends only to represent. By telling what and how we are supposed to know, it must exclude the forms of knowledge that would be improper. To achieve this, it must appear to discover the very propriety which it is its purpose to establish and sustain. The maxim teaches a knowledge which is also ignorance, not only a representational ignorance of particular instances of the improper, but of the way in which the commonplace is constitutive of this distinction it pretends to reflect and confirm. The magic trick is designed not only to achieve a certain end but, even more important, to conceal the way in which it achieves that end. If it fails in the concealment, the final result loses all appeal. If we discover that our brass replica of the Eiffel Tower was in fact made in Hong Kong from a mold sculpted from a drawing by someone who never saw the real thing and might not have known that such a thing or place existed, our fetishistic attachment to the souvenir may be transformed into an interest in the way in which that attachment occurred in the first place. (On the other hand, such a discovery might instead inspire an even more voracious wish to procure an authentic signifier. Such a reaction might stand comparison with the response of some critics to poststructuralism.) No positive answer may be adduced to this questioning which would not also enact the tautological self-grounding of any self-proclaiming truth. And yet the questioning itself in the first place—insofar as it is positively conceived or stated (as it must be, to be understood, to be viable even as a question)—must be limited in the same way, must foreclose certain possibilities of response, of conception, at the same time that it points out the way in which a prior knowledge imparted ignorance. No knowing can be communicated without simultaneously imparting an equal measure of not-knowing. The commonplace in this sense can only give way to a new commonplace which repeats the same error as its predecessor but, one hopes, with an ever increasing consciousness of doing so, an increasing sense of irony with respect to its own undertaking.

By now we have seen that certain issues cannot be avoided, if the phenomenon of aphoristic writing is to be closely addressed. Most generally these involve memory, pedagogy, and originality, all subsumed by subjectivity. Scrutiny of the aphorism reveals a failure, despite powerful efforts, to make an effective distinction between the manner, style, and matter, the content, of a formal literary enunciation. We have already seen one instance of this (Cicero, II, 313). Here is another interesting one from Quintillian:

> Does eloquence owe more to nature or to education? The ideal orator must be a blend of both. I believe the average orator owes more to nature, while the perfect orator owes more to education; just as good land will produce without cultivation, but really rich land will do best by cultivation. Praxiteles could have carved a statue out of a millstone, but Parian marble even in the rough would look better. (I, 108)

Again, this paradox which illustrates the fallaciousness of the distinction depends upon making the distinction in the first place. The metaphor of the sculptor, of artistic achievement, raises the issue of originality with particular force. The student's achievement here is the teacher's originality. It is the teacher who sculpts. So that the only positive originality that the student partakes of would appear to be someone else's—rather like Franklin's Poor Richard Saunders. Still, the metaphor of shaping, of turning one form into another through the same matter, provides a paradigm for the way in which originality is seen to occur. It occurs, let us note, as a function both of matter and of form, a contamination and an aporia of the two, and there are three principal metaphors used to develop it, art being the first.

Digestion, the ingestion of nourishment, is another of these metaphors.

For my part, if just now I were to want a complete novice trained up to oratory, I should rather entrust him to these untiring people, who hammer day and night on the same anvil at their one and only task, for them to put into his mouth none but the most delicate morsels—everything chewed exceedingly small—in the manner of wet nurses feeding baby-boys. (Cicero, I, 315)

Memory is the gastric juice in question here, and while nourishment must initially be sought in the originality of others, the proper assimilation of the other (in the text) will lead to a capacity for self-nourishment by the student. If the student assimilates (violates) the originality of the other text, using the commonality of the original's (common) place to make it *his* place, then he achieves an originality of his own.

I strongly approve of writing compositions as good for boys, but memorizing passages from orators or historians or other works is a much better practice than memorizing their own compositions. The best writings of the best authors are the necessary models for style; for they show the best words and the best art, while opening the treasure house of notable sayings, most useful in pleading cases because they carry the weight of authority. Occasionally boys may be allowed to declaim their own compositions, but only when they have polished off an unusually good one, which therefore merits a hearing. (Quintillian, I, 85)

The student thus acquires the ability to nourish his own mind, to feed on himself. This can occur only if he is to be at once both subject and object, and neither. The concept of originality is thus defined in terms of its own supercession. An original text is one which nourishes, that is, which gives rise to new original texts, new instances of originality, of the common place becoming indistinguishable from the first place (originality). The common place and the origin(-al) are intimately connected, each producing, being grounded in, and leading back to the other, making both at once possible and impossible. The clearest instance of their virtual coincidence would be the originality of the writer of maxims such as La Rochefoucauld, a producer of "original" commonplaces. This very aporia is the commonest place of all, and therefore the first place of all common places, and so neither first nor common.

The third recurring metaphor used in the description of originality in the use of commonplaces is translation. This figure merely de-

velops and repeats the same paradox as that of cannibalistic ingestion, dismemberment, and rend(er)ing of the original commonplace,
so that its originality is confirmed by the apparent dependence on
it, and erased by its assimilation, violation, and repetition.

> For my part, in the daily exercises of youth, I used chiefly to set
> myself that task which I knew Caius Carbo, my old enemy, was wont
> to practise: this was to set myself some poetry, the most impressive
> to be found, or to read as much of some speech as I could keep in
> my memory, and then to declaim upon the actual subject-matter of
> my reading, choosing as far as possible different words. But later I
> noticed this defect in my method, that those words which best be-
> fitted each subject, and were the most elegant and in fact the best,
> had been already seized upon by Ennius, if it was on his poetry that
> I was practising, or by Gracchus, if I chanced to have set myself a
> speech of his. Thus I saw that to employ the same expressions prof-
> ited me nothing, while to employ others was a positive hindrance,
> in that I was forming the habit of using the less appropriate. After-
> wards I resolved,—and this practice I followed when somewhat
> older,—*to translate freely Greek speeches of the most eminent or-
> ators.* The result of reading these was that, in rendering into Latin
> what I had read in Greek, I not only found myself using the best
> words—and yet quite familiar ones—but also coining by analogy
> certain words such as would be new to our people, provided only
> they were appropriate. (Cicero, I, 105–6)

Every original text must be grounded in the commonplaces, that
is, it must contain or allude to a commonplace, be able to be translated into one. What is good or useful about a text is defined in
terms of its capacity to compel a really objectless repetition, a recognition, reenactment, and failure of the idea of originality. Jane
Gallop has isolated, in the writings of the Marquis de Sade, a particularly graphic version of the digestive metaphor, but one admi-
rably suited to illustrate the nature of the commonplace in the original text, the way in which the original text achieves its originality
only through a repetition, by reading, of what is irreducibly common in it. Excrement is one thing we all have in common, a physical, irreducible common denominator, and it is the one part of our
bodies that cannot be altered through consumption and digestion by
a physical other, even ourselves. It is inassimilable, irreducible, and
therefore original, yet it is absolutely the commonest physical place
there is.

The turd is the dead moment fallen out of the digestive process. To eat it is to incorporate that which has already been detached (Bataille's pieces from Blanchot). Coprophagia can only reincorporate the fallen turd into the entire digestive process in the mode of an endless repetition ("the monotony which results from this sort of abuse"). The turd digested comes out turd, leaving nothing behind. The process of negation that the body operates on food in which food is negated dialectically (that is, retained and sublated) draws nothing from the turd. The turd will not be *aufgehoben*. (Gallop, 47)

Neither will the aphoristic text.

And yet, as Walter Benjamin points out in a quite different context, any literary text, any story, if it is any good, must lead to, translate into, and harbor in its guts an epigrammatic kernel of excrement: "All this points to the nature of every real story. It contains, openly or covertly, something useful. The usefulness may, in one case, consist in a moral; in another, in some practical advice; in a third, in a proverb or maxim" (86). A moral, practical advice, and a proverb or maxim are all the same thing—commonplaces. The question, especially in light of my discussion, becomes; Are these useful in a really pragmatic, literal rather than literary sense? Benjamin echoes many contemporary critics who would object to discourses like my own in saying that this divorce of aphorism or commonplace from usefulness, of literature from a utilitarian pragmatism, represents a break with tradition.

In every case the storyteller is a man who has counsel for his readers. But if today "having counsel" is beginning to have an old-fashioned ring, this is because the communicability of experience is decreasing. In consequence we have no counsel either for ourselves or for others. After all, counsel is less an answer to a question than a proposal concerning the continuation of a story which is just unfolding. To seek this counsel one would first have to be able to tell the story. (Quite apart from the fact that a man is receptive to counsel only to the extent that he allows his situation to speak.) Counsel woven into the fabric of real life is wisdom. The art of storytelling is reaching its end because the epic side of truth, wisdom, is dying out. This, however, is a process that has been going on for a long time. And nothing would be more fatuous than to want to see in it merely a "symptom of decay," let alone a "modern" symptom. It is, rather, only a concomitant symptom of the secular productive forces of history, a concomitant that has quite gradually removed narrative from

the realm of living speech and at the same time is making it possible
to see a new beauty in what is vanishing. (86–87)

Lewis P. Simpson, as astute and paradoxical a metaphysician of
history as Benjamin himself, reaches a similar conclusion with respect to American literary history.

> American society today does not conceive literacy to be a central
> need in the maintenance of civilizational order. The motive of lit-
> erary alienation—the keeping alive of "the spirit of the letter"—is
> draining away. This is not to say that poets, storytellers, and critics
> are disappearing, only that writing no longer centers in literature.
> The dominion of literature is effectively gone. (254–55)

And yet the very classical notion of the commonplace, and the
dependent idea of originality, seem to imply that the usefulness of
the story, of literature, has never been anything but an odd pleasure
in which both Benjamin and Simpson partake above, a pleasure which
is the apprehension of ongoing, irrecuperable loss, a beauty which
is viable aesthetically only as long as it is perceived as vanishing.
The "story which is just unfolding" is history itself, and history
itself is both more and less than what empiricists and pragmatists
might wish it to be—nothing but "a proposal concerning the continuation of a story," not simply an answer to a question, *the* question, but an answer which repeats the question and thus confesses
its own futility. History is this ongoing peregrination, dialogue, discourse, through the common and the first (original) places, which
of course are the same but somehow different. So history is literary
history. This is no less true in the present age. The dominion of
literature has always been gone, lost, and thus constituted as lost-
ness. And the loss of literature, the loss of history, their apocalyptic
beauty, has been going on—*has* to have been going on—since there
has been literature or history. Otherwise, Benjamin could not, would
not say that "death is the sanction of everything that the storyteller
can tell" (94). What seems so oddly paradoxical—yet so predictable
in the light of my previous discussion—is that Benjamin should be
describing something which depends on death as really about to be
dead itself, once and for all. In fact his own discussion must, as
mine has, lead to the contrary answer (which is a question). The
original, the strong text, must contain the excrement of its own un-
doing, a commonplace, another text, transcending and deconstruct-

ing all subjectivity and objectivity. This is the purest instance of literary tradition, and it is most plainly visible in aphoristic writing.

It is thus no accident that deconstructive texts tend often to include many instances of aphoristic writing, and that they also show a predominant concern with the rhetorical commonplaces, categories, of the classical authors I have been discussing. "Rhetoric," writes Paul de Man, "radically suspends logic and opens up vertiginous possibilities of referential aberration" (*A o R,* 10). De Man, probably the most rigorously exemplary of deconstructive critics and arguably the purest, is also the one whose writing most tends to aphoristic formulation. Others have noticed this, as for instance Geoff Bennington. "*Allegories of Reading* is a collection of tempting epigraphs, a work full of aphorisms waiting to be turned into slogans" (84). Unfortunately, Bennington and others have failed to understand why this should be the case. Thinking to have exposed de Man's fatal weakness (not moving "beyond a simplistic level of pseudo-wisdom"), what in fact they have discovered is the classical nature of deconstruction. De Man's aphoristic statements are of a very particular semantic nature, and self-descriptive even as they are self-erasing: Each is a small, self-contained text which "deconstructs its own performance," "a *text* in that it allows for two incompatible, mutually self-destructive points of view [that of the zealous believer and that of the appalled critic, as Bennington very correctly describes] and therefore puts an insurmountable obstacle in the way of any reading or understanding" (*A o R,* 131).

It is not hard to recognize here an epistemological pessimism akin to that of La Rochefoucald but even more like the maturely self-destructive pronouncements of Chamfort. De Man can approach the essence of the text (its aphoristic unreadability) only by enacting it, by framing it through repetition. One may be either entertained or enraged by this self-avowing legerdemain. Here is another prime example:

A text such as the *Profession de foi* can literally be called "unreadable" in that it leads to a set of assertions that radically exclude each other. Nor are these assertions mere neutral constatations; they are exhortative performatives that require the passage from sheer enunciation to action. They compel us to choose while destroying the foundations of any choice. They tell the allegory of a judicial decision that can be neither judicious nor just. As in the plays of Kleist, the verdict repeats the crime it condemns. If, after reading the *Profession de foi,* we are tempted to convert ourselves to "theism," we stand convicted of foolishness in the court of the intellect. But if we decide that belief, in the most extensive use of the term (which must include all possible forms of idolatry and ideology), can once and forever be overcome by the enlightened mind, then this twilight of the idols will be all the more foolish in not recognizing itself as the first victim of its occurrence. (*A o R,* 245)

Often the epigrammatic tension inscribed in these textural black holes attains to lyrical extremities. They could have been written by a certain kind of poet. (De Man taught in similar fashion: meticulous readings which would abruptly turn pyrotechnically lyrical). One of the very best examples is consigned to a footnote, scrutinized in the previous chapter, which ought to be famous, if it is not: "We do not see what we love but we love in the hope of confirming the illusion that we are indeed seeing anything at all" (*Diacritics,* 33n).

Rhetorically, what is happening in the last case is a chiasmus of verbs, but not simply that. A pure chiasmus would give: "We do not see what we love, but love what we see," or "we do not see what we love, but love in order to see." This is not nearly as potent as what de Man gives us. "In the hope of confirming the illusion" is what creates the aphoristic tension of the sentence and also what makes it so exemplary, not just for de Man but for the commonplace tradition. For de Man as for Proust (and I would even say for all literate persons), desire and writing sooner or later become figures for one another, and writing, like desire, always reflects the hope of confirming an illusion. As Proust puts it in his equally aphoristic formulation: "Dreams are not realizable, we know this; we wouldn't have any, perhaps, if it weren't for desire, and it is useful to have some so as to see them fail, and so their failure may instruct" (Proust, III, 378; my translation). There is in the tradition of aphorism a tension between on the one hand hope and confirmation, which fuel the endless repetition of inscription, and on the other hand a self-awareness of the Pyrrhic nature of writing (and desire), a consciousness that any writing at all depends on self-delusion, a false hope, in order to be read or written. Even people who know better buy postcards, take pictures, sometimes even vandalize monuments. Even once the impasse which is language, thought, has been recognized, it can be described only by repeating it, framed only by enacting it.

There is, in deconstructive literature, a most exemplary instance of this which I shall try to narrate—to repeat. Shoshana Felman has encapsulated what Jacques Lacan saw in Poe's story, "The Purloined Letter," which by now has so affected the reading of that text in the minds of so many readers as to become the story itself.

> What Lacan is concerned with at this point of his research is the psychoanalytic problematics of the "repetition-compulsion," as elaborated in Freud's speculative text, *Beyond the Pleasure Principle*. The thrust of Lacan's endeavor, with respect to Poe, is thus to point out—so as to elucidate the nature of Freudian repetition—the way in which the story's plot, its sequence of events (as, for Freud, the sequence of events in a life-story), is entirely contingent on, overdetermined by, a principle of repetition that governs it and inadvertantly structures its dramatic and ironic impact. (135)

The particulars of Lacan's argument are not what interests me, but rather the way in which Poe's story, through Lacan, has functioned as a kind of commonplace machine or "*machine à aphoriser*", the vortex of which would have to be the purloined letter itself: an empty, unknown, an unknowable locus of illegitimate substitution, purloinment. The repetition allegorized by the story depends on impropriety. The hope of substitution, of repetition, is always improper, an illusion. The repetition of the commonplace, the statement of a supposedly universal truth, is pure impropriety, and Lacan himself draws our attention to the way in which the epigrammatic genre perfectly enacts this innate property of the signifier.

> And to elaborate on Chamfort, whose formula that "one may bet that every public idea, every received convention is a stupidity, because it has pleased the greatest number," will surely please all those who believe they have escaped its law, that is to say precisely the greatest number.
>   . . . Isn't the prestidigitator (Dupin in the story, and Poe himself) repeating his trick in front of us, without deceiving us this time about telling us his secret, but pushing his bet here to the very point of really exposing it to us without our seeing a thing? This would surely be the greatest achievement of the illusionist, to *truly delude* us by one of his fictive creations. (30–31; my translation)

Note carefully what Lacan does with Chamfort's original commonplace, for it is precisely what he does with Poe's text, precisely what Derrida later does with this text of Lacan, and precisely what Barbara Johnson later does with them all. He takes Chamfort's severely paradoxical, anticommonplace commonplace and frames it in words of his own, elaborating, repeating, enacting a kind of *mise en abîme* of the double bind inscribed in it. Appearing to reverse the opposition according to which Chamfort's text functions (common wisdom / uncommon wisdom), showing how Chamfort, as textual prestidigitator, appears to exempt himself from the very logic on which his statement depends, Lacan can avoid incriminating himself along with Chamfort as "stupid" only by repeating the latter's prestidigitation. Lacan himself is caught in the very double bind he describes, and which effectively combusts his text as surely as it does Chamfort's. Derrida, commenting on Lacan, will repeat the same gesture (Johnson, *CD,* 110–46). And Barbara Johnson, finally, has no choice but to end her analysis by repeating the aphoristic double bind inscribed in the Poe story: "What is undecidable," she writes, "is whether a thing is decidable or not." And of course we are back to Chamfort, for if nothing is decidable, then we cannot even decide that nothing is decidable. "The sender again receives his own message backward from the receiver" (*CD,* 146).

It is the very same sort of impropriety, prestidigitation, in unison with a feint at candor, which has enabled me to say that all reading and all writing, and I would even say all desire, come down to repetition, to the illusory totalization of the aphoristic commonplace. For as I said in the first part of this chapter, the very notion of a common place is improper, enacts a logical impropriety, an aporia. There are no real commonplaces. They are only, at best, working assumptions. By acting as though they existed, we produce, as if by magic, certain effects, signs, substitutions for them by which their absence is supplemented. So to say that all writing, all desire and understanding, come to commonplace is to say they all come to nothing. Which must apply to the previous sentence as much as to any.

5

Aphorism and Fable:
La Fontaine and
Joel Chandler Harris

It will appear crazy to some, and offensive to just as many, to mention Joel Chandler Harris, the creator of Uncle Remus, in the same breath with the French poet and fabulist Jean de La Fontaine—Harris, apologist for the antebellum South, for slavery, patentee of the ultimate white fantasy of the adoring, passive, blissful-in-abjection black man who recounts tales of "Brer Rabbit" in pathetically endearing, illiterate dialect, alongside one of the great masters of French classicism and all its resources of irony, paradox, and every manner of literary subterfuge. But to justify such a comparison, the two need have no more in common than the genre of fable.

While a great deal of critical attention has been lavished on the resources of fable in La Fontaine's literary practice, no comparable scrutiny of rhetoric and genre in Harris' work has ever been attempted. Harris' undertaking in the Uncle Remus tales is conditioned at least as much by properties innate to the genre of fable as it is by a pseudoanthropological and apologist intention and a particular set of circumstances in American history. Illuminated by insights gleaned from La Fontaine, Harris' work appears more complex but is also seen more clearly. His differences from La Fontaine are all the more instructive because of what the two bodies of work have in common. What becomes apparent is a much more paradoxical view of the black man than anyone has realized, and a much more complicated attitude toward literature on the part of nostalgia-stricken white Southerners like Harris.

Fable is, generically, a particular kind of allegory, one in which animals, plants, and sometimes even inanimate objects speak and act as though human. This is a classic illustration of the dictionary definition of allegory: "speaking otherwise than one seems to speak." And allegory, as Angus Fletcher has pointed out, is very close to the meaning of irony: "saying one thing and meaning another." The irony is in the service of a moral, or maxim, with which every fable is supposed to conclude, and for which it serves as an illustration. From the outset, the genre is a kind of trickery. Its message pertains to men, but is conveyed through the acts and speech of animals which cannot in reality speak or walk upright. The maxim, the raison d'être of every fable, does not apply to animals but to men. This is very far from a direct imitation of reality, and it ought to be reserved for moments of extreme subtlety, when there is an imperative to expression which cannot declare its meaning, source, or intention directly. The genre of the maxim itself, incorporated if only by implication in that of the fable, enacts a similar self-contradiction: It must be particular, grounded in detail, and yet reflect the most universal truth; it must be original (clever), inventive, and yet create the sense in a reader of having always been true. *Maxima sententia*: the greatest truth in the smallest space. So, as we have seen, maxim is always paradox, an algebra of oppositions (universal / particular, commonplace / original, truth / fragment) in which the essence is neither of the terms opposed, but rather the tension of their very fine discrepancy. If that noncoincidence disappears, the maxim becomes a cliché and loses its force. The goal of every maxim, as an original statement, must not be to eliminate this tension but rather to increase it. So the fable, from beginning to end, from animals speaking and wearing clothes to the kernel of wisdom at the end, is nothing but irony and paradox.

It is not at all accidental that in France the fable and the maxim reached the highest point of their development at the same time, during the reign of Louis XIV, in the works of La Fontaine and La Rochefoucauld. The indirection of the two genres served both to lure and to foil the scrutiny of a repressive political regime. To lure, by the possibility of commentary or even advice to the monarch concealed under the inscrutable lamination of allegory, which would of course excite the keenest attention, reading, and rereading by those in power. To foil because, if handled properly, irony and al-

legory will never stop leaping back and forth across the gap of their
ambiguousness, will never deliver plainly in a neat package the content occulted by the same rhetorical gestures which sustain the illusion of that content's presence and its virtual accessibility. The
idea is to convince the reader that there really is a content there,
just out of reach, which one more careful reading might reveal,
while making sure that such a resolution of ambiguities is impossible. This is true not only for the purposes of avoiding censorship
and purloining some measure of power (that of seduction, the power
of the story to command a furrowing of brows among the truly powerful), but also for the literary quality of the fable or maxim. The
greater, the more subtle the irony, the better, the more effective,
the more original these are seen to be. Louis Marin has written in
Le Récit est un piège:

> In its desire for power, power will always listen to the fable as if it
> controlled the secret of knowing (end, code, meaning), of Truth which
> would make power absolute—that is, without any left over, without
> exteriority. And the storyteller—if he is clever—will always allow
> to appear a residue that must be guessed at, invented, which makes
> all knowledge (and truth) uncertain. That means this, but also that,
> and maybe even something else. Thus power—and the knowledge
> of power—disperses itself by its very desire for power in fables and
> stories. Thus does it lose its time in appearances; thus is it diverted
> by amusement; thus does it play like a child. "Why should one won-
> der / That the soundest reasoning / Fatigued often from lack of
> sleep /Should take pleasure in nodding, cleverly rocked / By tales
> of Ogre and Fairy?" (33–34; my translation)

Joan DeJean, another recent reader of La Fontaine, has said that
"the dazzling surfaces of Classicism constitute a brilliant machine
for controlling all readers, for keeping them in the dark, for dis-
couraging them from asking questions about the identity of the master artist who surrounds them with '*dorures*' and who caresses them
when the lights are out" (109). One would have trouble finding a
more precise metaphor for the fabulist's position, since his power
is conditioned on his disappearance, his invisibility. The identity of
La Fontaine exists only in what he says, and so is subjected to the
same play of irony, paradox, and allegory. Like a puppeteer dressed
entirely in black, his presence is known only by its erasure, the
illusion of its absence, the mirage of these animals talking and act-

ing like men, these sentences which throw back the reader's scrutiny like polished metal surfaces. This disappearance *is* power, the only real power accessible within a realm of absolutism to anyone but the monarch. Even the king's underlings have no power of their own but only what he lends them. The fabulist's power comes from his respect for language, for its unreliability, its power to deceive even the most powerful and the most astute. It is not a power purchased by linguistic pragmatism, except insofar as words must be used to seduce a reader's attention, but by a wariness of the traps within language—the possibility of being misunderstood (understood positively) in a dangerous fashion, of being caught in a seditious gesture of rhetoric, intended or not. This wariness appears to the audience / reader as an inscrutability, a purposeful concealment of some valuable, positive thing to be known—a secret.

Some readers of La Fontaine would have it that such a secret is actually delivered, whole, by each fable. This can be true only if one admits, with the critic Ross Chambers (in contradiction with his own reading of La Fontaine), that "there are no secrets." According to this view the secret is part of the allegorical illusion of the fable and does not exist. As the maxim or point of each fable, it is of course "delivered"—but as what? Ironic paradox, a statement which calls itself into question, erases its positiveness even as it is disclosed. So the "'interest' of the fable" cannot be pedagogical, as Chambers calls it, unless one conceives of and espouses the teaching of ignorance, something not reflected in his conclusion. The secret which he sees being disclosed in a fable about secrecy is the most severe irony, pure oxymoron: "Et je sais même sur ce fait / Bon nombre d'hommes qui sont femmes" ("And I even know of, on this matter / A good number of men who are women.") For me, at least, it is difficult to agree with Chambers' construal of such a facetious paradox as liberationist polemic.

All this calls for illustration. Here is a well-known short fable of La Fontaine. Marianne Moore's translation gives a good sense of the original's ironically lapidary language.

Certain Renard gascon, d'autres disent normand,
Mourant presque de faim, vit au haut d'une treille
    Des raisins murs apparemment,
    Et couverts d'une peau vermeille.
Le galant en eut fait volontiers un repas;

Mais comme il n'y pouvait atteindre:
"Ils sont trop verts", dit-il, "et bons pour des goujats".
Fit-il pas mieux que de se plaindre?

A fox of Gascon, though some say of Norman descent,
When starved till faint gazed up at a trellis to which grapes were tied—
    Matured till they glowed with a purplish tint
    As though there were gems inside.
Now grapes were what our adventurer on strained haunches
    chanced to crave
    But because he could not reach the vine
He said, "These grapes are sour; I'll leave them for some knave."
Better, I think, than an embittered whine.

"Norman" and "Gascon" here are figures for two apparently quite contradictory attitudes toward language. The Norman, somewhat like the New Englander in American popular folklore, is always reluctant to commit himself; "repondre en norman" ("to reply as a Norman") means to reply equivocally: "maybe yes, maybe no." On the other hand, the Gascon uses language to assert himself with utmost fervor. Synonyms listed in the *Petit Robert* are *fanfaron* and *hableur,* "blusterer," "braggart." So, as I am indebted to Ross Chambers for pointing out, the fable is equivocating between and extolling both ambiguity in language ("Norman") and the outright and deliberate conflation of language with reality ("Gascon")—in the fox and in itself. Even so, the crux of the matter is not the fox's provenance, but vision distorted by hunger. In the French, the word *apparemment* appears prominently in the description of the grapes. What is at stake here is perception, appearance, even if *apparemment* is understood to mean "obviously," "evidently," rather than "apparently," on account of the word's emphatic placement, after rather than (as usual) before the adjective *murs.* Either way, the mediation of perception is invoked. Because the fox is "starved till faint" and the grapes are above him, with the light (one supposes) shining through, they look to him to be perfectly ripe. That perception may or may not be accurate. The attempt to reach the grapes fails, and the fox uses language to change the nature of the grapes, making them unworthy of his desire. Desire first embellishes an object visually and then, when frustrated, denigrates it to diffuse the frustration. At both stages a drama of representation is enacted in which the object itself is not much more than pretext. Because of a physical imperative (hunger, a particular instance of desire), the fox first sees the grapes as desirable and then, because gratification is blocked, negates that first perception. Language is a response to the frustration of desire, of consumption. The fox will never know if the grapes were really ripe or not, and neither will the reader. The fox's response to this suspension of knowledge is a commentary on the grapes, by which he achieves a certain mastery over his desire and the circumstances.

What follows—the maxim or secret of the fable—is only half given to us by the narrator. Just what is better than complaining, than an "embittered whine"? To denigrate the grapes, of course, but this conclusion is left to the reader. When one cannot verify supposition (are the grapes ripe?) grounded in desire, it is better to diffuse the desire by revising the supposition than to embrace and give voice to frustration. Yes, but this is too evident. What can the narrator be alluding to? The first line led us to suppose a specifically human, perhaps ethnologic, content. What might it be, beyond the two apparently contradictory attitudes toward language already alluded to? Is not our situation, as readers, rather like the fox's? We have supposed something about the words of the fable because of our desire to know its meaning. At the end there is no revelation save the banal assertion—which we are left to complete—that it is better to denigrate an object that is out of reach than to pursue it futilely. This is cliché, something we already knew. What greater meaning might be implied?

The last line of the fable does not stop our wondering, as this reading demonstrates. As readers of the fable, we do not follow the fox's example, even though we see it as commonplace. Ought we not, if the wisdom here is so evident, to do as the fox does and denigrate the fable? Yet we do not. We continue to read fables and to be puzzled by this one. The narrator has enacted an allegory which shows his readers their own lack of wisdom in continuing to read him, in not diffusing their own desire to know what the allegory of the fable means, to confirm a supposition about it. The clear implication, according to this reading, is that we, the readers, are fools. But the narrator will not confirm this supposition either. He derives a power over us from two things: our hunger to know what he means, and his own absence from the fable, his refusal to declare himself, his intentions. His voice, like every literary voice, is without a subjectivity attached which we might interrogate about intentions and origins. Just as the fox's (and the fable's) origin and linguistic strategy are in doubt ("Gascon" or "Norman"?), so the fable is cut off from any sure intention, origin-ality, authorial authority. Could the real meaning of this fable be that men do not do what they ought to do, even when they know and recognize the wisdom of the right action? Perhaps. In inventing new endings, commentaries, codas for the fable, we do follow the fox's example after a fashion, responding to the frustration of our desire to know with language, with revised suppositions, though these do not entirely negate the ones we began with. These revisions, instead of diffusing our desire completely, only defer it, master it for a moment and then give way to fresh wonderings, a more subtly directed desire to know. And of course the fox does not diffuse his hunger either by saying that the grapes are sour. He simply redirects it, frees it for new suppositions, new objects. There is something both Norman and Gascon about this process, embracing as it does the ambiguousness of language (its "Norman" aspect) and its power to affect or overwhelm reality (its "Gascon" side).

What is illustrated here is just what astute readers of La Fontaine—Louis Marin most notably—have pointed out before: the power of the fabulist, the power of dissimulation, allegory, irony. That power is just as much at stake in the Uncle Remus tales as in La Fontaine, but perhaps even more interestingly, for the fabulist himself (Remus) has become part of the fable. He appears and is visible, but within the framework of fable this appearance cannot be more than a veil, an illusion cloaking the truth of his character—a truth which the fable conceals and empowers by diffusion. That he should be black is not a matter of choice to Harris as his author, but still the fact is coincident with certain aspects of the fable, and of color, in a sufficiently pregnant way to have charged Harris' imagination, albeit unconsciously. Black is a color which by definition connotes both absence and surfeit of visible light, invisibility and overvisibility. The fabulist is just this sort of absent presence, cloaked in shadow to sustain the illusion of his allegorical voices and shapes. He "caresses" his audience "when the lights are out," as Joan DeJean puts it. What, and who, is the audience of Uncle Remus? A white boy. The fabulist here is a literal darkness, a shadow, at the opposite end of the visible spectrum from his listener. Yet white is also defined as both "achromatic" and "perceived to belong to objects that reflect diffusely nearly all incident energy throughout the visible spectrum," free from color and yet reflecting every color. So teller and listener are each a mirror image, a reversal, of the other, and the blackness of Remus reflects (*sic*) a certain chromatic potential for blankness, for obscurity, disappearance, and power which is latent in the white child who listens to him. The boy's attention is compelled by something which, as a (chromatic) figure, reverses him, achieving in the process the power of the fabulist, maker of maxims.

Harris' fable is thus an allegory of fable, a fable of fable itself, in which both teller and listener are engulfed in the ambiguous lesson of the tale. This lack of a clear distinction between the levels of representation within the story is established by Harris as something emanating from the "dark presence" of the black storyteller.

. . . the old man [spoke] in a tone which implied that he was quite prepared to believe the dream was true. "Many's and many's de time, deze long nights en deze rainy spells, dat I sets down dar in my house over ag'in' de chimbly-jam'—I sets dar en I dozes, en it seem lak dat ole Brer Rabbit, he'll stick he head in de crack er de do' en see my eye 'periently shot, en den he'll beckon back at de yuther creeturs, en den dey'll set dar en run over de ole times wid one er n'er, en crack der jokes same ez dey useter. En den ag'in," continued the old man, shutting his eyes and giving to his voice a gruesome intonation *quite impossible to describe,*—"en den ag'in hit look lak dat Brer Rabbit'll gin de wink all 'roun, en den dey'll tu'n in en git up a reg'lar juberlee. Brer Rabbit, he'll retch up and take down de trivet, en Brer Fox, he'll snatch up de griddle, en Brer B'ar, he'll lay holt er de pot-hooks, en ole Brer Tarrypin, he'll grab up de fryin' pan, en dar dey'll have it, up en down, en 'roun' en 'roun'. Hit seem lak ter me dat ef I kin git my min' smoove down en ketch up some er dem ar chunes w'at dey sets dar en plays, den I'd lean back yer in dish yer cheer en I'd intrance you wid um, twel, by dis time termorrer night, you'd be settin' up dar at de supper-table 'sputin' 'longer yo' little brer 'bout de 'lasses pitcher. Dem creeturs dey sets dar," Uncle Remus went on. "en dey plays dem kinder chunes w'at moves you fum 'way back yander; en many's de time w'en I gits so lonesome kaze dey ain't nobody year um ceppin' it's me. Dey ain't no tellin' de chunes dey is in dat trivet, en in dat griddle, en in dat fryin'-pan er mine; dat dey ain't. W'en dem cree-

turs walks in en snatches um down, dey lays Miss Sally's pianner
in de shade, en Mars John's flute, hit ain't nowhars."

"Do they play on them just like a band, Uncle Remus?" inquired
the little boy, *who was secretly in hopes that the illusion would not
be destroyed.*

"Dey comes des lak I tell you, honey. W'en I shets my eyes en
dozes, dey comes en dey plays, but w'en I opens my eyes dey ain't
dar. Now, den, w'en dat's de shape er marters, w'at duz I do? I des
shets my eyes en hol' um shot, en let um come en play dem ole time
chunes twel long atter bedtime done come en gone." (185–86; emphasis mine)

The most interesting difference from the fables of La Fontaine
may be the stance of Harris himself. He has projected the voice of
the fabulist—his own voice—into the fable and into the figure of
a black man. Harris tries, in his preface to the stories, to describe
his role as that of an amateur anthropologist, a folklorist, taking
great pains to authenticate the tales as African in origin and to pho-
netically capture the dialect of the black storyteller. His relation to
his fables, to literature, is thus highly ambiguous, and represented
as identical to his relation with the black man. The black storyteller
is the narrative representation of that ambiguity toward the indeterminacy, the power of literature, which Harris is compelled to enact,
but from a distance, to enact and deny at once. His purpose has
always been assumed, by himself and his critics, to be the glori-
fication of antebellum plantation society.

If the reader not familiar with plantation life will imagine that the
myth-stories of Uncle Remus are told night after night to a little boy
by an old Negro who appears to be venerable enough to have lived
during the period which he describes—who has nothing but pleasant
memories of the discipline of slavery—and who has all the preju-
dices of caste and pride of family that were the natural results of the
system; if the reader can imagine all this, he will find little difficulty
in appreciating and sympathizing with the air of affectionate superiority which Uncle Remus assumes as he proceeds to unfold the
mysteries of plantation lore to a little child who is the product of
that practical reconstruction which has been going on to some extent
since the war in spite of the politicians. (xxvi–xxvii)

Harris represents the black man as quaint, comical, endearing,
but ignorant; the stories Remus tells, though sophisticatedly ironic,

are phrased in the language of an illiterate though charming dialect. The power of literature is represented here as illiterate, and knowledge and education (whiteness) are shown as incompatible with that power (blackness, literature) to which the white writer is drawn inexorably, but which he is compelled to project outside himself into an otherness of obscurity and anachronism. Yet the act of Harris' writing, like the rapt attention of the little boy in the stories, confirms that power even as it thrusts it away in the guise of a specifically racial otherness.

The heretofore ignored significance of these stories is that, in them, the mentality of nostalgic postbellum Southerners like Harris is represented, and it turns out to be rather peculiar in ways one might not have expected. In every one of these tales is an allegory of the educated, conservative white Southerner's view of race relations, and he appears to be less sure of his superiority than has been assumed. The same allegory represents the white Southerner's relation to literature as equally complex: As any publisher can attest, the region has always been the least hospitable to the best writing, even when it comes from the pens of natives. Science, accuracy, a soberness with regard to fact and history, are embraced by Harris. These, at least, are of practical value. Fable, literature, the word wielded for its own sake, for nothing but the pleasure it can give—and the power, but this is not so apparent—are projected into the black man's face and voice. Or rather they are simply assumed to belong there. But it must always be remembered that, in this way, the black man is denigrated for the very same reason that the fox libeled his grapes— because of his distance, his status as the holder of a secret which he will not reveal, which makes him an object of frustrated desire and empowers him to dispense pleasure in small doses. He is disparaged for his power of words, a power of darkness latent in the white man, but which the white man alienates from himself so that he may have the pleasure of being seduced by it and of bludgeoning it with a disdain born of fear. For to wield that power directly is to embrace, to disappear into the power of the literary word, the indeterminacy of allegory.

In the Remus corpus there is a fox-and-grape story which serves perfectly as a point of comparison with La Fontaine. Entitled "How Brother Fox Failed to Get His Grapes," it begins with a wry evocation by the narrator of the black man's quaint suspicion, grounded in ignorance, of newfangled medical science.

One night the little boy failed to make his appearance at the accus-
tomed hour, and the next morning the intelligence that the child was
sick went forth from the "big house." Uncle Remus was told that it
had been necessary during the night to call in two physicians. When
this information was imparted to the old man, there was an expression upon his countenance of awe not unmixed with indignation. He
gave vent to the latter:

"Dar now! Two un um! W'en dat chile riz up, ef rize up he do,
he'll des nat'ally be a shadder. Yer I is, gwine on eighty year, en I
ain't tuck none er dat ar doctor truck yit, 'ceppin' it's dish yer flas'
er poke-root w'at ole Miss Favers fix up fer de stiffness in my j'ints.
Dey'll come en dey'll go, en dey'll po' in der jollup yer en slap on
der fly-plarster dar, en sprinkle der calomy yander, twel bimeby dat
chile won't look like hisse'f. Dat's wat! En mo'n dat, hit's mighty
kuse unter me dat ole folks kin go 'long en stan' up ter de rack en
gobble up der 'lowance, en yit chilluns is got ter be strucken down.
Ef Miss Sally'll des tu'n dem doctor mens loose onter me, I lay I
lick up der physic twel dey go off 'stonish." (177–78)

This demonstration of the old man's hopelessly primitive understanding is juxtaposed with a description of his slavish devotion to
his white folks, the Victorian mawkishness of which is impressive.

Every night after supper Uncle Remus would creep softly into the
back piazza, place his hat carefully on the floor, rap gently on the
door by way of announcement, and so pass into the nursery. How
patient his vigils, how tender his ministrations, only the mother of
the little boy knew; how comfortable and refreshing the change from
the bed to the strong arms of Uncle Remus, only the little boy could
say. (178)

Uncle Remus' visits make the boy's "term of imprisonment . . .
full of pleasure," the pleasure of blackness, of storytelling: "Almost
the first manifestation of the child's convalescence was the renewal
of his interest in the wonderful adventures of Brother Rabbit, Brother
Fox, and the other brethren who flourished in that strange past over
which this modern Aesop had thrown the veil of fable" (178).

What is the strange past referred to here? Some antediluvian age
of fantasm in which rabbit and fox wore clothes and spoke—one
in which the gap between myth and reality was closed and also, by
implication, that between representation and truth, literature and
science, black and white? That strange past is created by the "veil
of fable" thrown over it by the black storyteller. Harris says in his
introduction that the mythic time alluded to is no more remote than

the years before the Civil War: "the myth-stories . . . are told by an old Negro who appears . . . to have lived during the period which he describes" (xxvii). The prelapsarian age in question can be none other than the Southern antebellum years. The old black man, strong yet quaintly ignorant, adept with words but fearful of science, is the only remaining link with that age of fable. This gives him both his power and his weakness, the strength of myth and the frailty of obsolescence. It is as though no clock had begun to tick until the defeat of the South, no grim seconds counted till the gray uniform had been amply blood-spattered and ripped. Remus survives as a fading remnant of that magical age, the last of a race of wizards whose powers are always fading but never disappearing, always ambiguous because his being is past, a discrepancy with the present and even with time. Remus is a bit of the hypothetical mythic reality before there was time, of a reality which never was (when slaves were happy and loved servitude and every white master was serenely benevolent), of untime, fallen into the dross of temporal existence. So he is always in danger of disappearing completely, of becoming invisible. His language, so archaic, so ungrammatical, incompatible with the science of grammar, risks becoming unintelligible. But this threat of disappearance *is* his power, as the only remaining bond with a past outside of time. Of course the little boy would rather float in the giddy firmament of darkness, of untime, in the arms of the old black man, than on the clammy white sheets of his very real and medicinal bed.

As for the story itself, it deals with the power of words over perception, but in a more pointed, subtly aggressive way than La Fontaine's version. Brother Rabbit and Brother Fox find themselves rivals for the attention of the same gaggle of women in the neighborhood. Whether rabbit, fox, or some hybrid, the species of these females is never specified. We must understand them to partake of a golden age in which differences of genus did not count for nearly so much as nowadays. Brother Rabbit—the perpetual underdog, with no weapon at his disposal but language—decides to humiliate his competitor in the only way he can. He tells Brother Fox about a bunch of grapes he has seen.

"'I wuz takin' a walk day fo' yistiddy,' sezee, w'en de fus' news
I know'd I run up 'g'in' de bigges' en de fattes' bunch er grapes dat

I ever lay eyes on. Dey wuz dat fat en dat big,' sezee, 'dat de nat'al juice wuz des drappin' fum un, en de bees wuz a-swarmin' atter de honey, en little ole Jack Sparrer en all er his fambly conneckshun wuz skeetin' 'roun' dar dippin' in der bills,' sezee.

"Right den en dar," Uncle Remus went on, "Brer Fox mouf 'gun ter water, en he look outer he eye like he de bes'frien' w'at Brer Rabbit got in de roun' worl' . . .

" '. . . Dey er dat ripe,' sez ole Brer Rabbit, sezee, 'dat dey look like dey er done melt tergedder, en I speck you'll fin' um full er bugs, but you kin take dat fine bushy tail er yone, Brer Fox,' sezee, 'en bresh dem bugs away.'

"Brer Fox 'low he much 'blige, en den he put out atter de grapes in a han'-gallop." (180)

The rabbit has followed the example of La Fontaine's fox, but in order to manipulate the fox's desire, not his own. He has created, out of nothing but words and the slight resemblance between a bunch of grapes and another less palatable but very real object, a surrogate object of desire. He has, with words, made that object of desire appear so compelling that the fox chooses to pursue it rather than "Miss Meadows and the gals." The rabbit has even given hints of his deceitfulness, which however only serve to make the illusion, the Fox's error, more effective. He warns the fox that that the grapes will be full of bugs. In fact, "Dem ar grapes all so fine wuz needer mo' ner less dan a great big was'-ness', en dem bugs wuz deze yer red wassies" (181).

Remember that the black man and the little boy are just as much within the realm of fable as the fable itself. What the rabbit does with the larger, more dangerous fox is just what the black man does for the boy: to invent out of words an illusory object of desire, the story of the fox, the rabbit, and the grapes. That story demonstrates the power of language to deceive, to manipulate, and to humiliate even an adversary who has every apparent advantage of force. And the old black man, though he does not subject the white audience to humiliation, certainly does manipulate, deceive him, deception and verbal manipulation being the very essence of successful storytelling. The latent possibility of humiliation is sketched very graphically, however, with the implication that it could be used, if necessary. The boy submits to this control because, like La Fontaine's reader, he wants the secret of knowledge, to feel the mythical

wholeness before the fall into defeat and time, which for him and
for Harris is represented by the pre–Civil War South.

That the Old South of Harris and many other postbellum white
Southerners' nostalgia should be fable, a sort of prelapsarian myth,
is not as surprising as that the guardian of that myth should be a
black man. Still, one might object, that black man is a white fantasy, the most flaccid of Uncle Toms. But reading him alongside
La Fontaine shows at least that Uncle Remus is not the helpless,
doting Negro that even his author tries to make him into. If the black
man is to sustain the fable of the Old South—by dissimulation,
irony, and all the resources of the fabulist—he must have the fabulist's power. This is a power which is not granted. It must be
acquired by anyone who would wield it, and it can be achieved only
through verbal elusiveness. If the white child, or Harris, takes pleasure in the black man wielding this power of narration over their
greater resources of force, this does not mean that he is their creature, any more than La Fontaine can be called the creature of Louis
XIV and his minions. It is by appearing to gratify a need to know,
a nostalgia for pure knowledge, fabulous origin, in the only way
that these can be gratified—by trickery, deferment, an endless series of supplements and substitutions for the absence of any such
knowledge, the infinite invention of new, always ephemeral objects
of desire—that the black man in the South of Harris' childhood, or
the man of letters in seventeenth-century France, compels a superior
political force to respect him. If Remus is a white fantasy, he is not
one which disparages the black man. Very much the contrary. Remus is the embodiment of literature. The white Southerner, with his
condescension to literature and blackness (the former prejudice has
perhaps survived intact to a greater degree than the latter), with his
confusion of the two, is the one who appears in a bad light, sitting
raptly open-mouthed at the feet of an uneducated black man, beg-
ging for another tale.

The consequence of white positivism, of expecting a real, definitive answer to all questions, is illustrated in the story of the tar-
baby. Because the tar-baby (a man- or fox-made simulacrum of a
Negro) will not speak to him, the rabbit strikes it, trapping himself,
losing all freedom of movement. Of course the tar-baby was a trap
set by the fox to catch the rabbit. To entrap his tormentor, the fox
makes a false fabulist, a black man. This tar-baby inspires a com-

pulsion to know, to hear words spoken, on the part of the rabbit. Because the tar-baby cannot give the rabbit what he demands (respond to his greeting), appearing to withhold it, the rabbit becomes frantic, finally surrendering all privilege of unencumbered motion, all dignity of superior intellect, becoming stuck in the gooey obscurity of an Uncle Remus, a made-up fable-spinner. He regains his power only by realizing his error and playing tar-baby to the fox. He tells his captor that the torture he most fears is to be thrown into a briar patch. Hearing this, the fox throws him right away into the nearest one. The rabbit, to whom there is no friendlier element than briars, sashays off home. The dark power of words can be escaped only by embracing it, something which Harris will do only at a distance in the persona of Remus, fantasy though he may be.

There is considerable evidence, though, that Harris' depiction of the black is not fantasy, beyond assertions by nostalgia-struck simpletons delirious with age who declare, "Why yes, the niggers was just like that in the old days, back on the plantation!" Many prominent blacks have embraced old Remus, among them the critic Henry Louis Gates. Uncle Remus is nothing but a white man's translation of the black figure of the "signifying monkey."

The Signifying Monkey is a trickster figure, of the order of the trickster figure of Yoruba mythology, Esù-Elégbára in Nigeria, and Legba among the Fon in Dahomey, whose New World figurations—Exú in Brazil, Echu-Elegua in Cuba, Papa Legba in the pantheon of the *loa* of Vaudou in Haiti, and Papa La Bas in the *loa* of Hoodoo in the United States—speak eloquently of the unbroken arc of metaphysical presuppositions and patterns of figuration shared through space and time among black cultures in West Africa, South America, the Caribbean, and the United States. These trickster figures, aspects of Èsù, are primarily *mediators*: as tricksters they are mediators and their mediations are tricks.

The versions of Èsù are all messengers of the gods: he interprets the will of the gods to man; he carries the desires of man to the gods. He is known as the divine linguist, the keeper of *àse* ("logos") with which Olódùmarè created the universe. Èsù is guardian of the crossroads, master of style and the stylus, phallic god of generation and fecundity, master of the mystical barrier that separates the divine from the profane world. In Yoruba, Èsù always limps, because his legs are of different lengths: one is anchored in the realm of the gods, the other rests in the human world. The closest Western relative of

Èsù is Hermes, of course: and, just as Hermes' role as interpreter
lent his name readily to "hermeneutics," the study of the process of
interpretation, so too the figure of Èsù can stand, for the critic of
comparative black literature, as our metaphor for the act of interpretation itself . . .

     . . . Unlike his Pan-African Èsù cousins, the Signifying Monkey
exists in the discourse of mythology not primarily as a character in
a narrative but rather as a vehicle for narration itself. It is from this
corpus of mythological narratives that signifying derives. The Afro-
American rhetorical strategy of signifying is a rhetorical practice
unengaged in information giving. Signifying turns on the play and
chain of signifiers, and not on some supposedly transcendent signified. Alan Dundes suggests that the origins of signifying could "lie
in African rhetoric." As anthropologists demonstrate, the Signifying
Monkey is often called "the signifier," he who wreaks havoc upon
"the signified." One is "signified upon" by the signifier. (687–89)

To "signify" can mean, in Afro-American usage, to make fun of
someone or simply to display great verbal virtuosity, talking a great
deal and never saying anything identifiable as a content. This is just
what Uncle Remus does. Even if Remus is a white fantasy, a tar-
baby set up by Harris for the pleasure of signifying on himself, he
is still a surprise. Who would have thought the myth of the Old
South depended above all else on the figure of a black man? It may
be going too far, but one might wonder, given the real changes that
have occurred in the way the black man is seen by the white South,
and the concurrent decline in zeal for the age of Southern glory, if
we might not expect literature to find more widespread and profound acceptance in the region.

6

Aphorism and Modern Poetry:
The Advent of the Antimaxim

Aphorism never held an important place in American letters until recently—a circumstance owing to a particular historical consciousness, or rather to the lack of any. The twentieth century, indeed, bears ironic comparison with the grand age of the maxim in Europe. Moralistic epigrams flourished in France from La Rochefoucauld in the seventeenth century to the lesser known Chamfort at the end of the eighteenth, so that the reign of Louis XIV and the French Revolution mark the limits of the age of aphorism. Thereafter the aphorism did not try to stand as a genre on its own but hid in the convolutions of essay and poem, where it lurked, implike, until in twentieth-century poetry it reemerged, perhaps paler and stranger, but nonetheless stronger than ever—aphorism, that is, understood as a pithy, quasi-sententious, or wisely nonsensical fragment. And it may be that American poets now have an edge on continental ones, in that they lack a moralistic, aphoristic tradition. No La Rochefoucauld peers imaginarily over their shoulders. This has allowed American writers to embrace the antimaxim perhaps more fervently, less agonistically, and so has allowed it to become a characteristically American rhetoric. My point here is not the banal assertion that there are aphorisms in modern poetry, but that poetry has in fact become, to a considerable degree, an aphoristic genre.

The golden age of aphorism in France coincided with the dying gasp of a certain concept of history, of temporality, which allowed a fragment to stand on its own because it was assumed to refer back to a wholeness which could not be apprehended otherwise, just as the present was understood, as a fragment, to fit into an immutable tapestry of time on which past and future were matters only of perspective, and of which each stitch, of whatever shape or color, told some truth. This is in essence an antihistorical stance, for it allows no possibility of progress or of significant change in the course of human events. This was the view represented by the Ancients in the famous quarrel in France's literary community at the end of the seventeenth century. Bossuet, Boileau, and others of the party of the Ancients hewed to the view of Saint Augustine, a view which is wholly subjectivistic as to time, but which insists on an objective truth visible to the Deity and which men may only infer, through the bits and pieces of their illusory, subjective experiences.

> O God, grant that men should recognize in some small thing like this potter's wheel the principles which are common to all things, great and small alike. There are stars and other lights in the sky, set there to be *portents, and be the measures of time, to mark out the day and the year* . . .
>
> It is in my own mind . . . that I measure time. I must not allow my mind to insist that time is something objective. I must not let it thwart me because of all the different notions and impressions that are lodged in it. I say that I measure time in my mind. For everything which happens leaves an impression on it, and this impression remains after the thing itself has ceased to be. It is the impression that I measure, since it is still present, not the thing itself, which makes the impression as it passes and then moves into the past. When I measure time it is this impression that I measure. Either, then, this is what time is, or else I do not measure time at all . . .
>
> What is true of the whole psalm is also true of all its parts and of each syllable. It is true of any longer action in which I may be engaged and of which the recitation of the psalm may only be a small part. It is true of a man's whole life, of which all his actions are parts. It is true of the whole history of mankind, of which each man's life is a part . . .
>
> But it is unthinkable that you, Creator of the universe, Creator of souls and bodies, should know all the past and all the future merely in this way. (Augustine, 271, 276, 278, 279–80)

So the concept of history as a science which could reveal objective truth was seen—and logically proved—by Augustine to be false. The truth of human events and human nature is immutable, and the history of that truth from a human perspective is a fabric of imperfect, distorted, illusory perceptions grounded in the hallucination of temporal, postlapsarian experience. Men stumble, only half-seeing, through the illusion of time, toward the end of that illusion, toward the City of God. Chronology reflects a fall from perfection into imperfection which, as it compounds itself, piling illusion on illusion, moves toward immolation and closure. In this view as in classical antiquity, the maxim reflects the immutable truth visible only by fragments, in the disjointed apprehension of human foible. Each bit of human experience, though illusory, may be refined by reason (the link with divine knowledge) so that, as a thread or fragment, it infers the design of the whole cloth, the Logos from which it fell.

If the temporal sequence of that experience reflected any story at all, it was one of decay. The cyclical theory propounded by the Englishman George Hakewill and on the continent by Jean Bodin and Machiavelli, to name a few, was more optimistic only in the short term. Still, it did begin to conceive history, time, as more than a delusional passage downward punctuated by the abrupt verticality of salvation or damnation. Later, in the seventeenth century, the Moderns in France laid the groundwork for a view of history as ascent, while the scientific advances of such individuals as Descartes, Bacon, and Newton seemed to substantiate such a view. The scientific revolution of the time tended toward a secularization of knowledge and encouraged the view that human perception in general was much more than illusion. So that, throughout the seventeenth century, there is a discernible movement from the essentially antihistorical, Augustinian view of temporality (that of the Ancients) toward one which saw the present as at least equal and probably superior to the past. Charles Perrault, a leader of the Moderns, wrote: "I am convinced that, if the ancients are excellent, as can scarcely be denied, the moderns nevertheless yield to them in nothing and even surpass them in many things" (92). But if the Moderns in this debate believed that progress was possible, they did not believe that human nature could change. In this, at least, they remained Augustinian. Fontenelle, a Modern, wrote:

> Men change their dress, but not the form of their bodies. Politeness, coarseness, knowledge or ignorance . . .; all these are no more than the outside of mankind; and these indeed change. But the heart does not change, and the essence of man is in the heart . . . Among the prodigious number of irrational men born in any span of a hundred

years, nature produces perhaps thirty or forty rational . . . I leave
you to judge if they are to be found anywhere or at any time in
numbers sufficient to bring virtue and integrity into fashion. (quoted
in Baumer, 135)

Even someone so modern in outlook as Nicolas de Malebranche,
a Cartesian, called history "a false science." So that while the tendency was toward a historical consciousness, history continued to
be called an illusion by virtually all parties to the debate between
Ancients and Moderns, and the maxim continued to flourish as a
sort of supplement for the absence, the inaccessibility, of the "whole"
story (history). Nevertheless the Moderns, in their positivistic conception of knowledge, their refusal to accept the Augustinian view
of history as a secret knowable only to the Deity, of temporality as
a delusional consequence of the fall, provided the basis for an argument in favor of secular history. And sure enough, in the eighteenth century Gibbon would call history "the science of causes and
effects." Giambattista Vico considered history a science superior in
objectivity to all the physical sciences. Through it,

> there will then be fully unfolded before us, not the particular history
> in time of the laws and deeds of the Romans or the Greeks, but (by
> virtue of the identity of the intelligible *substance* in the diversity of
> their *modes* of development) the ideal history of the eternal laws
> which are instanced by the deeds of all nations. (414–15)

Chamfort's aphoristic pessimism appears as an anachronism in
this context. He held on to a degenerative view of time which, while
secular, retained the aspects of classical and Augustinian thought
necessary to make the maxim a more valid expression of human
truth in time than any more direct effort to discern the whole behind
the fragment.

> Physical scourges and calamities of human nature have made society
> necessary. Society has added to the miseries of nature. The ill con-
> sequences of society have led to the necessity of government, and
> government adds to the miseries of society. This is the history of
> human nature. (64; my translation)

But Chamfort was the very last of the great writers of maxims, and
his attitude toward history belonged more to the seventeenth century
than to the eighteenth in which he lived and wrote.

The nineteenth century saw an apogee of historicism. Hegel, Marx, Taine, Zola, and J. S. Mill all participated in the general conviction that "this earth is no longer a vale of tears," at least potentially. "The riches of divine life," wrote D. F. Strauss, "are to be realized right here and now" (quoted in Baumer, 336n). No dent would be inflicted in this historical positivism until the twentieth century, nor would there be any revival in the practice of the epigram in literature. As long as there existed a faith in the power of men to "predict the future" (Winwood Reade, quoted in Baumer, 336), to see the whole of human time, the fragment could not be viewed as a necessary access to the totality of truth. This was the age of the monolith in literature, the effort to reproduce "scientifically" all of human nature and knowledge in fiction or poetry, an impulse evident in Zola's *Les Rougon-Macquart,* Hugo's *La Légende des siècles* and Balzac's *Comédie humaine*.

All this was to change most drastically. In 1927 the Prussian minister of culture, C. H. Becker, wrote that "the age of historicism is over . . . Faith in objective historical thought has disappeared" (Baumer, 500). And the Englishman Michael Oakeshott elaborated five years later: "The distinction between history as it happened (the course of events) and history as it is thought, the distinction between history itself and merely experienced history must go; it is not merely false, it is meaningless" (93). With World War I and the discoveries of relativity and the uncertainty principle by Einstein and Heisenberg, a new attitude toward history set in, one much like that of the seventeenth-century Ancients, but with a difference: the revived Augustinian view of temporality as illusion is thoroughly and completely secular. Heidegger's existential model of time is remarkably like Augustine's. In *Sein und Zeit* he defines the moment (*Augenblick*) as purely negative, the fall of the future into the past. But Heidegger does not, at least early on, countenance the possibility of some sort of duration grounded in divine spirituality. His version of time is unlike Augustine's in this very radical way: Here we see pure flux, mutability, the negativity of the moment cut off from a Logos (whether science or the Deity) which could impart stability on any level. The difference between science as Logos and the Deity as Logos had been the difference between an age of fragment and an age of wholes (history). The divine logocentrism of the Ancients is more like the Logosless twentieth century because the Deity was not thought to be accessible to mortal man, while scientific truth was.

The outcome is that we begin to see, not as an independent genre but usually in poems, lapidarily succinct formulations which much resemble aphorisms. This is at least as true of American as of French verse. The present age may be viewed as America's first real chance to write in the epigrammatic mode; American poets have been free to invent their own aphoristic tradition. Perhaps this is why their language, their metaphors, are less strained, less severely contrastive than those of the French, who must work harder to distance themselves from an older tradition. One finds in French poetry such epigrams as this one by Max Jacob: "On connaît bien peu ceux qu'on aime / mais je les comprends assez bien / étant tous ces gens-là moi-même / qui ne suis pourtant qu'un babouin" (*Penguin Book of French Verse,* 567). ("One knows very little of those one loves / but I understand them well enough / being all those people myself /who am however only a baboon.") This one by Paul Eluard may be more typical: "C'est la chaude loi des hommes / Du raisin ils font du vin / Du charbon ils font du feu / Des baisers ils font des hommes" (*Penguin,* 616). ("This is the hot law of men / From the grape they make wine / From coal they make fire / From love-making they make men.") In America, meanwhile, there was Stephen Crane: "You say you are holy, / And that / Because I have not seen you sin. / Ay, but there are those / Who see you sin, my friend." Crane's very brief texts seem to combine rhetorical traits of both fable and maxim: "A man feared that he might find an assassin; /Another that he might find a victim. / One was more wise than the other" (*Mentor Anthology,* 228–29). The difference, of course, is that here there is no pretense to deliver a positive truth. Wallace Stevens displays a similar penchant for the aphoristic figure: "Life consists of propositions about life . . . / The whole race is a poet that writes down / The eccentric propositions of its fate." The reality of this poetry, as Stevens wrote, is a "dimension in which / We believe without belief, beyond belief" (*Mentor,* 286). Once again, the conviction emerges that life is a "a fragmentary tragedy / Within the universal whole" (Stevens, *Mentor,* 303).

And what is that whole? Something entirely unknown, even more inaccessible than the Deity to the seventeenth-century Ancients. Something in which, as Stevens put it, "We believe without belief, beyond belief." The seventeenth-century closure of apocalypse, union with the divinity, end of illusion, is replaced by the belief in a finitude imposed on every fragment, on all time, by nothing more than nothingness. It is the *absence* of any transcendental truth that gives these fragments their truth, their beauty. The French poet Francis Ponge has written one of the most succinct elaborations of this sort of closure.

> Et puis après la fin de tout le règne animal, l'air et le sable en petits grains lentement y pénètrent, cependant que sur le sol il luit encore et s'érode, et va brillamment se désagréger, ô stérile, immatérielle poussière, ô brillant résidu, quoique sans fin brassé et trituré entre les laminoirs aériens et marins, ENFIN! *l'on* n'est plus là et ne peut rien reformer du sable, même pas du verre, et C'EST FINI! (*Penguin,* 625)

> And then after the end of the entire animal kingdom air and sand in small grains slowly penetrate it, yet on the ground it still shines and wears away, and is going brilliantly to disintegrate, O sterile, immaterial dust, O brilliant residue, though endlessly turned and ground between the aerial and marine rollers, FINALLY! *One* is no longer there and can reform nothing from the sand, not even glass, and IT IS FINISHED!

The epigram is no longer esteemed for achieving the greatest meaning in the smallest space (*maxima sententia*), but for its capacity to convey the violence of the absence of meaning. And indeed the name of epigram—meaning "writing upon, an inscription"—is now more apt than that of maxim. The new aphorism is not engraved on any bedrock but left to flutter in thin air like smoke. Maurice Blanchot has summed up the new fragmentary aesthetic in discussing one of its most prominent French adherents, René Char.

> Fragment: it is difficult to approach this word. "Fragment," a name, but having the force of a verb, yet absent: break, broken without debris, interruption as word when the stoppage of intermittence does not arrest the process of becoming but on the contrary provokes it into the rupture which belongs to it. Whoever says fragment must not only say fragmentation of an already existing reality nor moment of a wholeness yet to come. This is difficult to consider because of the exigency of comprehension according to which there is knowledge only of the whole, just as vision is always a whole view: according to this understanding, it would be necessary that wherever

there is a fragment, there is a subjacent indication of a wholeness
which was before or would be so again later—the amputated finger
referring back to the hand, as the first atom prefigures and contains
the universe. Our thought is thus confined between two limits, that
of the imagination of substantial integrity and that of the imagination
of dialectical becoming. But, in the violence of the fragment and,
in particular, that violence to which René Char gives us access, a
very different relation is given to us, at least as a promise and a task.
"What is reality without the dislocating energy of the poem?"
    . . . *Pulverised poem* is not a name which diminishes. *Pulverised
poem*: to write, to read this poem is to agree to fold the understanding
of language into a certain fragmentary experience, that is, one of
separation and discontinuity. (449–50; my translation)

A number of differences in style and content set the new fragment
apart from the old maxim. In French, the integrating pronoun *on,*
so ubiquitous in La Rochefoucauld, Vauvenargues, and Chamfort,
has become scarce. We have gone from La Rochefoucauld's "On
peut être plus fin qu'un autre, mais non pas plus fin que tous les
autres" (23) ("One can be more subtle than another, but not more
subtle than all the others") to Char's "Lie dans le cerveau: à l'est
du Rhin. Gabegie morale: de ce côté-ci" (104) ("Dregs in the brain:
east of the Rhine. Moral muddle: on this side") or "Je vois l'homme
perdu de perversions politiques, confondant action et expiation,
nommant conquête son anéantissement" (104) ("I see the lost man
of political perversions, confusing action and expiation, calling his
annihilation conquest"). In American poetry the words *time* and *history,* to which little attention was ever given by classical writers of
maxims, appear as an overriding obsession, as for instance in the
exemplary poet Robert Penn Warren: "And over the black stones
the rain / Has fallen, falls, with the benign indifferency / Of the
historical imagination, while grass, / In idiot innocence, has fin-
gered all to peace" (*Brother to Dragons,* 9); "If there were no
wind we might, we think, hear / The earth grind on its axis, or
history / Drip in darkness like a leaking pipe in the cellar" (*SP,*
5); "Time / Is only a mirror in the fun-house" (*SP,* 21); "history, / Like nature, may have mercy, / Though only by accident"
(*SP,* 105). Yet it should be clear from these examples that Warren's
history names an absence, celebrates a loss of faith. It is simply
wrong to read American literature as an attempt to establish a his-

torical identity in and through literature. The references to history, like the relative rarity of the pronoun *on* in Char, signify the loss of a Logos. The poem is perfectly aware of the impossibility and the meaninglessness of the concept of history, and supplements, substitutes for that loss by celebrating, naming it. "Time," Warren tells his reader, "is the mirror into which you stare," and therefore "you must re-evaluate the whole question" (*SP*, 21).

Why, then, has the fragment not taken on new life as a genre on its own? Why does it appear only in poetry, as poetry? Simply because there is no whole from which everyone might understand the fragment to have fallen, to lend integrity to each piece when it is read separately. Now, the fragment is embedded in larger fragments, in a tissue of fragments, fragmentary poems. We might call twentieth-century aphorisms fragments to the second power, realizing as they do a kind of reflexive fragmentariness, an irony of fragmentariness. Ironic, because indirect and indeterminate, not meaning what any aphorism had always seemed to mean—that there is a larger whole of truth to guarantee their integrity. Reference, signification, ricochets from fragment to fragment, from a line within the poem to the whole poem, using the means of the maxim to lead us, very deliberately, nowhere at all. This was of course a possibility always latent in the maxim. Never has it been so fully exploited as now, though Chamfort stretched the limits of classicism to flirt with it.

Both Char and Warren represent in poetry the changed view of history which has made a resurgence of aphoristic language possible. They have done so in an epigrammatic rhetoric which damns history rhetorically and thematically. Char included a piece called "Le Bouge de l'historien" ("The Historian's Hovel") in *Seuls demeurent,* poems written before and during World War II.

> La pyramide des martyrs obsède la terre.
> Onze hivers tu auras renoncé au quantième de l'espérance, à la respiration de ton fer rouge, en d'atroces performances psychiques. Comète tuée net, tu auras barré sanglant la nuit de ton époque. Interdiction de croire tienne cette page d'où tu prenais élan pour te soustraire à la géante torpeur d'épine du Monstre, à son contentieux de massacreurs.
> Miroir de la murène! Miroir du vomito! Purin d'un feu plat tendu par l'ennemi!

Dure, afin de pouvoir encore mieux aimer un jour ce que tes mains d'autrefois n'avaient fait qu'effleurer sous l'olivier trop jeune. (47)

The pyramid of martyrs obsesses the earth.

For eleven winters you shall have renounced the nth degree of hope, the breathing of your red iron, in atrocious psychical performances. A comet killed clean, you shall have fenced in and canceled, bloody, the night of your age. Prohibition of thinking your own this page from which you took the impulse to submit yourself to the enormous thorny torpor of the Monster, to its contentiousness of those who massacre.

Mirror of the moray eel! Mirror of vomit! Liquid manure of a flat fire / deceased repast proferred by the enemy!

Endure, in order to be able to love better one day what your archaic hands had only brushed beneath the too young olive tree.

Here the word "eleven" is juxtaposed with the infinity of the indeterminate "nth": its closure, the historian's impulse to reveal the totality of the story of time, is symbolized in the two straight lines, cut off top and bottom, of this completely vertical Arabic numeral. The frigid inhumanity of this rectilinear lust for closure is set off by the idiosyncratic use of the expression *quantième* (nth), which most commonly appears in the expression "Quel est le quantième du mois?" (What is the day of the month?). So it calls to mind human life at its most mundanely, quotidianly, curvilinearly human—and fragmented. This sort of question—which does not look beyond the moment, the unstable space of a day, and lives within the renunciation of totality that is what individual human lives are made of—is juxtaposed by omission with the historian's compulsion to totalize, to add things up, which cannot be escaped even by admitting the bankruptcy of historical positivism. The luridly hyperbolic fragments in which the poem is written, most of them perfectly exemplifying Barthes's formula for a classical maxim (NOUN / COPULATIVE / NOUN), are a rhetorical antithesis of the historian's journalistic prose. "Prohibition of thinking your own this page from which you took the impulse to submit yourself . . .": the historian's is a perverted poetical impulse, one stolen from the page of the fragmentary poem and from the fragmentary humanity of which the page of the poem is part, the larger page on which we all live. The only truth is this epigrammatical evanescence. The historian's wish to string such smokelike bits into a fabric of totality

reflects the only truth there can be in closure: death. This is why
the historian's prose reflects death, disease (vomit), night, the fanged,
phallic eel of putrefaction. Life, the stuff of poetry (beneath the
olive tree) is piecemeal. The poem, out of doors under the tree, is
an apostrophe to the historian, who is inside the decrepit structure
of his morbid words, so it is couched in a quasi-religious tone. The
poet /moralist's religion is, in stark contrast with his seventeenth-
century ancestors, one which refuses all integration.

An analogous text by Warren is the poem "History." This is a
small, dense excerpt:

> In the new land
> Our seed shall prosper, and
> In those unsifted times
> Our sons shall cultivate
> Peculiar crimes,
> Having not love, nor hate,
> Nor memory.
> Though some,
> Of all most weary,
> Most defective of desire,
> Shall grope toward time's cold womb;
> In dim pools peer
> To see, of some grandsire,
> The long and toothed jawbone greening there.
> (O Time, for them the aimless bitch
> —Purblind, field-worn,
> Slack dugs by the dry thorn torn—
> Forever quartering the ground in which
> The blank and fanged
> Rough certainty lies hid.)
> . . . .
> We seek what end?
> The slow dynastic ease,
> Travail's cease?
> Nor pleasure, sure:
> Alloy of fact?
> The act
> Alone is pure.
> . . . .
> We are the blade,
> But not the hand

> By which the blade is swayed.
> Time falls, but has no end.
> Descend! (*SP*, 295–96)

This text is written in the same pastiche of older religious writing
as Char's, a rhetoric of soberest, albeit ironic, prophecy. Who are
those who "grope toward time's cold womb" to see in the water a
vision of "greening" individual death—the "weariest" and "most
defective of desire"? Who but the historians? Time as they see it is
barren, its "womb" beckoning only the "blank and fanged / Rough
certainty" of death. They belittle time by projecting onto it their
wish for closure, a desire for death, making it into a starved, stray
canine pawing the earth for monstrous sustenance, more death. The
poet speaks for a different order of reality, a different temporality.
There is no end to his time; it "falls" forever, colliding with no
obstacle, no ending which might close it off. The "end," the "hand /
By which the blade is swayed" cannot be known, only the fragmentary act which "alone is pure," and which the poem's fragmentariness embraces by enactment.

An analogous poetic dismissal of historicity is evident in these
lines from Wallace Stevens' "Dutch Graves in Bucks County":

> And you, my semblables, are crusts that lie
> In the shrivellings of your time and place
> . . . .
> And you, my semblables, in the total
> Of remembrance share nothing of ourselves
> . . . .
> And you, my semblables, in gaffer-green,
> Know that the past is not part of the present.
> (237–38)

The past, here emblemized by the gravestones of Stevens' Dutch
ancestors, represents an unnarratable truth of "total remembrance,"
of closure which, as Warren put it, "alone is pure." This truth an-
nihilates human identity and the petty subjectivity of time by sub-
jecting them to a "profounder logic, / In a peace that is more than
a refuge, / In the will of what is common to all men, / Spelled
from spent living and spent dying." This truth, so far as we can
know from the vantage point of life, is not a continuous fabric of
cause and effect at all.

If the day writhes, it is not with revelations,
One goes on asking questions. That, then, is one
Of the categories. So said, this placid space
Is changed. It is not so blue as we thought. To be blue,
There must be no questions. It is an intellect
Of windings round and dodges to and fro,
Writhing in wrong obliques and distances,
Not an intellect in which we are fleet

(301)

Marianne Moore is another American poet who has denounced the pretentions of historical epistemology through a poetic of lightly ironic fragmentariness. In "'He wrote the History Book,'" her poetic voice sees far more truth in an offspring's description of a historian parent than in that parent's "mask of profundity": "You shed a ray /of whimsicality on a mask of profundity so / terrific, that I have been dumfounded by / it oftener than I care to say" (89). The truth is least of all in the historian's claim to wield it ("*The* book? Titles are chaff," replies the poet's voice to such pretentiousness); rather, it is in the momentary and quite unpremeditated words of a son or daughter, rendered all the more powerfully ironic and dismissive by their nearly random offhandedness: "you contribute to your father's / legibility and are sufficiently / synthetic. Thank you for showing me / your father's autograph" (89).

Allen Tate, in the most famous of all his poems, "Ode to the Confederate Dead," has damned history as a Pyrrhic narcissism in much the same terms as Warren: "Night is the beginning and the end / And in between the ends of distraction / Waits mute speculation, the patient curse / That stones the eyes, or like the jaguar leaps / For his own image in a jungle pool, his victim" (22). The contemporary poet Fred Chappell is typical in echoing the same sense that only death, the antithesis of historicity, can be real truth: "Unmoving in time, / only the dead are incorrupt. / / *Time I shall not serve thee*" (184).

The bankruptcy of history has given custody of truth back to the poet, then—truth, that is, defined negatively as the absence of transcendental meaning. The poetry of Char and of Warren, Moore, Stevens, Chappell, Tate, Ponge, Jacob, and many another poet in French and English celebrates fragmentariness, reaching beyond the historian's and the scientist's mourning for truth to a keen glee in contingency and instability. James Merrill has said as much very recently, testifying that the new age of aphorism is far from over: "Lost, is it, buried? One more missing piece? / But nothing's lost. Or else: all is translation / And every bit of us is lost in it / (Or found . . .)" (10).

7

Afterword

American writers have tended to represent the means of moralistic discourse, its voice and rhetoric, as an otherness: witchcraft, blackness (an enslaved and therefore safe alterity). Moralistic genres have traditionally been embraced only in the mode of an unquestioning repetition of pious cliché (Franklin), or in the twentieth century, when truth is no longer assumed to be an issue in aphoristic formulation at all. The only positive practice of aphorism in American letters which assumes its own veracity is Franklin's, and Franklin's truth is a truth of economic exchange. It reflects a theory of public welfare based on saving, abstention, avoidance of sensuality or, in Freudian terms, sublimation, and in literary terms, on a banality of sameness, of pious homily over and above any quest for a metaphysical truth or any interrogation into the grounding of such a truth.

American culture still esteems pragmatism of the sort exemplified in Franklin's Poor Richard above abstract inquiry into the nature and status of truth. Science, and indeed technology, are thought to be far more significant than literature, art, philosophy, or history. The nature and status of truth are not commonly regarded as important issues. Such is not at all the case in Europe, and the history of the various moralistic genres on both continents suggests why. One might object to this characterization by pointing to America's great legacy of freedom. Neither freedom of expression nor economic freedom, however, need be identical with a commitment to

105

serious intellectual inquiry. In America freedom developed and survived as an idea because it was consistent with, and indeed indistinguishable from, a certain economic system and set of historical circumstances. European liberties of expression and economy have been born of struggle, of violent conflict, both intellectual and physical.

It is a great paradox, then, that America and American literary critics should make such a strong claim to be moral, and denounce their continental counterparts (and countrymen contaminated by them) as amoral at best, immoral at worst. The American mind has tended to promulgate morality by repressing any possibility of a play within it, any possibility of manipulating its means of expression, through the intellectual equivalent of witchcraft trials or slavery. Literature today can play safely with the rhetoric of the maxim, because that rhetoric is no longer thought to have anything to do with the *veritas* of pragmatism, the economic system, technological progress, or growth in the GNP. Maximlike formulations, if not outright trivia, are museum pieces, expensive toys for bored dilettantes, harmless as dinosaur bones. The tradition of Franklin lives on in the myriads of self-help books and in television programs which address the same needs in the same spirit (*Wall Street Week,* for instance, or *Crockett's Victory Garden*). Americans are still "moral" only if that word is understood to connote devotion to certain homely pieties: home, family, God, country, individual and national prosperity. Literature in America has still not unironically or unreservedly embraced the pursuit, wherever it may lead, of an investigation of the rhetoric of truth, of authority, except in criticism, and there only beginning with the critical practice of a naturalized American, Paul de Man. If such critics as Geoffrey Hartman and Harold Bloom argue for a greater place in the literary canon for critical theory—even as, so ironically, they balk at what they see as de Man's "amorality"— this must be the reason why.

Works Cited

Aristotle. *The Poetics*. In *Aristotle, The Poetics, "Longinus," On the Sublime, and Demetrius, On Style*. Translated by W. Hamilton Fyfe and W. Rhys Roberts. Cambridge, Mass.: Harvard University Press, 1953.

Auden, W. H., and Louis Kronenburger, eds. *The Viking Book of Aphorisms*. New York: Viking, 1962.

Augustine. *Confessions*. Translated by R. S. Pine-Coffin. Harmondsworth, Eng.: Penguin, 1961.

Baumer, Franklin L. *Modern European Thought*. New York: Macmillan, 1977.

Benjamin, Walter. *Illuminations*. New York: Schocken, 1969.

Bennington, Geoff. "Reading Paul de Man." In *The Oxford Literary Review* 4:3 (1981): 83–93.

Blanchot, Maurice. *Le Livre à venir*. Paris: Gallimard / Collection Idées, 1959.

———. *L'Entretien infini*. Paris: Gallimard, 1969.

———. *L'Espace littéraire*. Paris: Gallimard / Collection Idées, 1955.

Brody, Jules. "La Bruyère: le style d'un moraliste." *Cahiers de l'Association Internationale des Etudes Françaises* 30 (1978): 139–54.

Chambers, Ross. "Histoire d'Oeuf: Secrets and Secrecy in a La Fontaine Fable." *Substance,* no. 32 (1981): 65–74.

Chamfort, Sébastien Roch Nicolas. *Eloge de Molière*. Paris, 1769.

———. *Produits de la civilisation perfectionnée: maximes et pensées, caractères et anecdotes*. Edited by Jean Dagen. Paris: Garnier-Flammarion, 1968.

107

Char, René. *Fureur et mystère*. Paris: Gallimard, 1967.

Cicero. *De Oratore*. 2 vols. Translated by H. Rackham. Cambridge, Mass.: Harvard University Press, 1942.

DeJean, Joan. "La Fontaine's *Psyché*: The Reflecting Pool of Classicism." *L'Esprit créateur* 21:4 (1981): 99–109.

de Man, Paul. *Allegories of Reading*. New Haven: Yale University Press, 1979.

———. *Blindness and Insight*. New York: Oxford University Press, 1971.

———. "Hypogram and Inscription: Michael Riffaterre's Poetics of Reading." *Diacritics* 11:4 (Winter 1981). 17–35.

———. "The Resistance to Theory." In *The Pedagogical Imperative,* Yale French Studies, no. 63 (1982): 4–20.

Edwards, Jonathan. *Images or Shadows of Divine Things*. Edited by Perry Miller. New Haven: Yale University Press, 1948.

Felman, Shoshana. "On Reading Poetry: Reflections on the Limits and Possibilities of Psychoanalytical Approaches." In *The Literary Freud: Mechanisms of Defense and the Poetic Will*. Edited by J. H. Smith. New Haven: Yale University Press, 1980.

Franklin, Benjamin. *Autobiography and Selections from His Other Writings*. New York: Modern Library, 1950.

———. *Papers*. Edited by Leonard W. Labaree and Whitfield J. Bell. 20 volumes to date. New Haven: Yale University Press, 1959– .

Gallop, Jane. *Intersections: A Reading of Sade with Bataille, Blanchot, and Klossowski*. Lincoln: University of Nebraska Press, 1981.

Gates, Henry Louis. "The 'Blackness of Blackness': A Critique of the Sign and the Signifying Monkey." *Critical Inquiry* 9 (1983): 685–724.

Graff, Gerald. *Literature against Itself*. Chicago: University of Chicago Press, 1980.

Harris, Joel Chandler. *The Complete Tales of Uncle Remus*. Boston: Houghton Mifflin, 1955.

Hawthorne, Nathaniel. *Novels*. New York: Library of America, 1983.

———. *Tales and Sketches*. New York: Library of America, 1982.

Hertz, Neil. "Two Extravagant Teachings." In *The Pedagogical Imperative: Teaching as a Literary Genre,* Yale French Studies, no. 63 (1982): 59–71.

Huizinga, Johan. *The Waning of the Middle Ages*. New York: Doubleday / Anchor, 1954.

Irwin, John T. *American Hieroglyphics*. New Haven: Yale University Press, 1980.

Johnson, Barbara. *The Critical Difference*. Baltimore: Johns Hopkins University Press, 1980.

———. "Teaching Ignorance: *L'Ecole des Femmes*." In *The Pedagogical Imperative,* Yale French Studies, no. 63 (1982): 165–82.

La Bruyère. *Les Caractères*. Edited by R. Garapon. Paris: Garnier, 1962.

La Fontaine, Jean de. *Fables*. Edited by Georges Couton. Paris: Garnier, 1962.

La Rochefoucauld, François de. *Maximes*. Edited by J. Truchet. Paris: Garnier, 1967.

Lacan, Jacques. *Ecrits I*. Paris: Editions du Seuil, 1966.

Lechner, Joan Marie. *Renaissance Concepts of the Commonplace*. New York: Pageant Press, 1962.

Lentricchia, Frank. *After the New Criticism*. Chicago: University of Chicago Press, 1980.

Lewis, Philip. *La Rochefoucauld, the Art of Abstraction*. Ithaca, N.Y.: Cornell University Press, 1977.

Lopez, Claude-Anne, and Eugenia W. Herbert. *The Private Franklin*. New York: Norton, 1975.

Marin, Louis. *Le Récit est un piège*. Paris: Les Editions de Minuit, 1978.

Mather, Cotton. *Selections from Cotton Mather*. Edited by Kenneth B. Murdock. New York: Hafner, 1926.

———. "The Wonders of the Invisible World." In *Narratives of the Witchcraft Cases, 1648–1706*. Edited by George Lincoln Burr. New York: Barnes and Noble, 1946.

Melville, Herman. *Moby-Dick; or, the Whale*. Edited by Harrison Hayford and Hershel Parker. New York: Norton, 1967.

The Mentor Book of Major American Poets. Edited by Oscar Williams and Edwin Honig. New York: New American Library, 1962.

Merrill, James. *Divine Comedies*. New York: Atheneum, 1977.

Moore, Marianne. *The Complete Poems of Marianne Moore*. New York: Macmillan / Viking, 1981.

Oakeshott, Michael. *Experience and Its Modes*. Cambridge: Cambridge University Press, 1933.

Pascal, Blaise. *Pensées*. Edited by L. Lafuma. Paris: Editions du Seuil, 1962.

The Penguin Book of French Verse. Edited by Brian Woledge et al. Harmondsworth, Eng.: Penguin, 1975.

Perrault, Charles. *Parallèle des anciens et des modernes en ce qui regarde les arts et les sciences*. Introduction by H. R. Jauss and M. Imdahl. Munich. Eidos Verlag, 1964.

Poe, Edgar Allan. *Works,* vol. 3. Edited by James A. Harrison. New York: AMS Press, 1965.

Poulet, Georges. "Chamfort et Laclos." In *Etudes sur le temps humain*. Paris: Plon, 1950.

Proust, Marcel. *A la recherche du temps perdu*. 3 vols. Edited by Pierre Clarac and Andre Ferré. Paris: Editions de la Pléiade, 1954.

Quintillian. *The Schoolmaster: The Institutio oratoria of Marcus Fabius*

Quintillianus. 2 vols. Edited, with English summary and concordance, by Charles Edgar Little. Nashville: George Peabody College for Teachers, 1951.

Rubin, Louis. "Robert Penn Warren: Critic." In *A Southern Renascence Man,* edited by Walter B. Edgar. Baton Rouge: Louisiana State University Press, 1984.

Simpson, Lewis P. *The Man of Letters in New England and the South.* Baton Rouge: Louisiana State University Press, 1973.

Starobinski, Jean. "Complexité de La Rochefoucauld." *Preuves* 135 (mai 1962): 33–40.

———. "La Rochefoucauld et les morales substitutives." *La Nouvelle Revue française* 163–64 (juillet–août 1966): 16–43, 211–29.

Symons, Julian. *The Tell-Tale Heart: The Life and Works of Edgar Allan Poe.* New York: Penguin, 1981.

Van Delft, Louis. "Qu'est-ce qu'un moraliste?" *Cahiers de l'Association Internationale des Etudes Francaises* 30 (1978): 105–20.

Vauvenargues. *Oeuvres choisies.* Edited by Pierre Chambry. Paris: n.p., 1968.

Vico, Giambattista. *The New Science.* Edited and translated by Thomas G. Bergin and M. Fisch. 3rd rev. ed. Ithaca, N.Y.: Cornell University Press, 1968.

Wallechinsky, David, et al. *The Book of Lists.* New York: Morrow, 1977.

Warren, Robert Penn. *Brother to Dragons.* New version. New York: Random House, 1979.

———. *Selected Poems, 1923–1975.* New York: Random House, 1975.

Index

Apthonius, 61–62
Aristotle, 4, 56, 63
Auden, W. H., 56
Augustine, 92–93, 95

Bacon, Francis, 93
Balzac, Honoré de, 95
Barthes, Roland, 5, 6, 100
Becker, C. H., 95
Benjamin, Walter, 69, 70
Bennington, Geoff, 71
Bercovitch, Sacvan, 36
Blanchot, Maurice, 45–55, 97–98
Bloom, Harold, 106
Bodin, Jean, 93
Boileau, Nicholas, 92
Bossuet, Jacques-Bénigne, 92
Brooks, Cleanth, 43
Brothers, Dr. Joyce, 23
Browning, Elizabeth Barrett, 39
Bunyan, John, 26–27

Carroll, Lewis, 63
Chambers, Ross, 78, 79

Chamfort, Nicholas-Sébastien Roch
    de, 10–17, 21, 52, 71, 73, 74, 91,
    94, 98, 99
Chappell, Fred, 103
Char, René, 97–101, 102, 103
Cicero, 57, 59, 62, 66
Crane, Stephen, 96

DeJean, Joan, 77, 81
De Man, Paul, 24–25, 35, 43–44,
    45–55, 71–72, 104
Derrida, Jacques, 25, 73, 74
Descartes, René, 93

Edwards, Jonathan, 26–27, 30, 31–
    33, 36, 39
Einstein, Albert, 24, 95
Eluard, Paul, 96
Erasmus, 4

Felman, Shoshana, 73
Fletcher, Angus, 76
Fontenelle, Bernard Le Bovier de, 93–
    94
Foucault, Michel, 25

Franklin, Benjamin/Poor Richard
    Saunders, 17–25, 66, 105–6
Freud, Sigmund, 105

Gallop, Jane, 68–69
Gates, Henry Louis, 89–90
Gibbon, Edward, 94
Graff, Gerald, 43

Hakewill, George, 93
Harris, Joel Chandler, 75, 81–90
Hartman, Geoffrey, 106
Hawthorne, Nathaniel, 37–39
Hegel, G. W. F., 9, 95
Heidegger, Martin, 95
Heisenberg, Werner, 24, 95
Hertz, Neil, 63
Hugo, Victor, 95

Irwin, John T., 36

Jacob, Max, 96, 103
Johnson, Barbara, 43, 64–65, 73, 74

Kazin, Alfred, 40
Kramer, Hilton, 40
Kronenburger, Louis, 56

La Bruyère, Jean de, 4–5, 6, 7–8, 9,
    30, 42
Lacan, Jacques, 73–74
La Fontaine, Jean de, 75–81, 83, 84,
    87, 88
La Rochefoucauld, François de, 4–7,
    8, 9, 12, 16, 17, 18, 52, 67, 71,
    76, 91, 98
Lentricchia, Frank, 43–44

Lewis, Philip, 5, 6, 17
Locke, John, 3
Louis XIV, 76, 91

Machiavelli, Niccolo, 93
Malebranche, Nicolas de, 94
Mallarmé, Stéphane, 47, 55
Marin, Louis, 77, 81
Marx, Karl, 95
Mather, Cotton, 26–27, 28, 29–31,
    32, 33–35, 36, 38, 39, 40, 41, 42
Melville, Herman, 39
Merrill, James, 104
Mill, John Stuart, 95
Miller, Perry, 36
Molière, 64–65
Moore, Marianne, 78, 103

Newton, Sir Isaac, 93
Nietzsche, Friedrich, 35

Oakeshott, Michael, 95

Pascal, Blaise, 26, 27–29, 31, 32, 35,
    36
Peale, Norman Vincent, 23
Perrault, Charles, 93
Peters, Dr. Lawrence, 23
Plato, 4
Poe, Edgar Allan, 38, 39–40, 73
Ponge, Francis, 97, 103
Poulet, Georges, 16
Proust, Marcel, 45–55, 58, 72

Quintillian, 61, 62, 63, 66

Ransom, John Crowe, 43
Reade, Winwood, 95
Rubin, Louis D., 41–42, 43, 44
Ruykeyser, Louis, 23

Sade, Marquis de, 68
Saunders, Poor Richard/Benjamin
   Franklin, 17–25, 66, 105–6
Shakespeare, William, 58
Simpson, Lewis P., 70
Starobinski, Jean, 5, 6, 17
Stevens, Wallace, 96–97, 102–3
Strauss, D. F., 95

Taine, Hippolyte, 95
Tate, Allen, 103
Theophrastus, 4

Vauvenargues, Luc de Clapiers,
   Marguis de, 5, 6, 8–9, 10, 98
Vico, Giambattista, 94

Wallace, Irving, et al., 23–25
Warren, Robert Penn, 42, 43, 98, 99,
   101–2, 103
Whitman, Walt, 58

Zola, Emile, 95